My souvenir to the
Rector's Office!
This is the beautiful
town where Mgr. Jessing
was born.

Tina Kroenberg

June 1981

The Old Town Hall in Münster
Engraving by J. Poppel from a drawing by J. F. Lange

JOSEF BERGENTHAL

MÜNSTER

CURIOSITIES AND TREASURES

WITH MORE THAN 100 ILLUSTRATIONS

VERLAG REGENSBERG · MÜNSTER

Translated by Sylvia Furness, Edinburgh
and five chapters (pages 123—133) by
Mary Junker-Brennan, Münster

ISBN 3-7923-0441-4

Third Edition 1979

CONTENTS

Münster! The very name of the town has a festive ring. The chanting of monks in the monastery about which the town grew up resounds in it, and the pealing of the bells which from here rang out their joyful message of peace to the world. The demoniacal cries of the Anabaptists have faded away like a distant echo, so has the storm of exploding bombs that smashed gables and vaultings and shook the very foundations of the town as if all houses should be levelled. Yet the terrible devastation did not completely crush the town. The darkened skies brightened again. The town which had been struck to the ground dragged herself painfully to her feet, rubbed the dust and dirt from her eyes and gathered her remnants of strength. Mux had been destroyed but life remained and bloomed again out of ruins. The stock of men which had created Münster is still living and, defying all the devastation, has built the town anew. Now, once again, we can walk through the old streets and lanes, across market places and along the ramparts and contemplate landmarks and monuments of art and architecture, ancient ruins and modern buildings. But anyone who wants to get to know the nature of this town really well, ought to know something of its historical past, the memory of which she still retains, he ought to enquire into those tales and legends which she herself stores in her memory, as a mixture of truth and fiction, historical reality and dreams in the mind of the people, he ought to interpret and understand the character of the people as it is expressed in custom and tradition, and ought always to be ready to recognise the significance and importance of some things which may lie inconspicuously by the roadside or even be completely hidden from view. Anyone who remembers these things as he walks with keen eyes through the old capital of Westphalia and her present-day life, will realize more clearly at each step that, in the words of Karl Wagenfeld, "the walls of Münster shelter much that is worthy of note".

The unforgettable picture recalling the beautiful old town of Münster.
This is the view from the Aegidii rampart across the town with its

many towers. During war-time bombing the old residential quarters
were destroyed, but the stalwart towers survived the great storm

Saint Liudger. Wood carving on a cupboard door in the Friedenssaal
(p. 32)

LIUDGER THE FOUNDER

Scarcely any information about Münster has come down to us
from olden times. When, at the beginning of the Christian era,
the Romans invaded the lands between the Rhine and the
Weser, and were defeated and thrown back by the Germanic
tribes, mention is made of the brave Bructeri, the tribe that
inhabited present-day Münsterland, but no mention is made of

any place which can be recognised as the later town of Münster. Almost eight centuries were to pass before Mimigernaford on the Aa in Saxony was to emerge into the light of history. This was at the period of the thirty years of conflict between Frank and Saxon, between Charlemagne and Widukind. Charlemagne fought this historic war in order to Christianize the Saxons and add their land to his own great Empire. Saxony at that time was difficult, even dangerous country. All around it, ambassadors of Christianity had succeeded in spreading their gospel of salvation among the Franks, the Hessians and even the Friesians. Only the Saxons continued to resist. So Charlemagne sent to them the Friesian priest Liudger as a missionary. Liudger won over West Saxony to Christianity and as a result his missionary diocese was elevated to a bishopric in 805, and he himself was ordained bishop. He was a Friesian of gentle birth and must have been a considerable personality. During his life and even after his death he exerted a great influence. A wealth of legends surrounds his memory. As church builder and patron saint, his name lives on up to the present day. He was the first bishop at the beginning of the history of the bishopric and of the town. His most important foundation is the Cathedral Church in Münster, with the Cathedral School, the present-day Paulinum, which claims the distinction of being the oldest grammar school in Germany.

THE BISHOP'S CASTLE

Liudger founded his mission on the Horsteberg in the ancient settlement of Mimigernaford. It was called *Monasterium*, the monastery; gradually its name evolved into Münster, while the old name went out of use. Around the Christian missionary settlement, to which the Cathedral Church, the houses of the clergy and the domestic buildings must have belonged, Liudger built a protective rampart and moat. Today the Cathedral area still stands out clearly from the rest of the town as its original nucleus. It can be recognised by the circle of streets enclosing the area along the curving line of the earlier ramparts, running through the Rothenburg, Prinzipalmarkt, Roggenmarkt, Bogenstraße and Spiekerhof. The four entrances to the Bishop's Castle are still there too, the former castle gates; Spiegelturm, Horsteberg, Michaelistor and Pferdegasse.

THE RAMPARTS

In the course of three centuries, increasing numbers of farmers, craftsmen and merchants settled round this Bishop's Castle. The bishops played an active part in politics. Several of them being Imperial Chancellors were visited by kings and emperors. But in 1121 Duke Lothar of Supplinburg conquered Münster. The citizens' quarter, the bishop's castle and the Cathedral were badly damaged by fire. After this the bishop decided it was necessary to build a rampart and moat which would protect the entire settlement and no longer only the area immediately round the cathedral. And so, in the middle of the 12th century, Münster's first rampart was built. A broad moat was dug in a wide sweep round the town, the earth was thrown up to form a rampart on the town side of the moat, and on top of this a strong wall with six defensive towers and eleven gates was built. Three centuries later, during the Soest hostilities, when an army of Bohemian mercenaries threatened to attack Soest and her allies, the rampart and moat were further reinforced. Later the Anabaptists completed the work on the great double rampart with its many towers and gates, entrenchments and rondels, and the town was believed to be impregnable. But in the Seven Years War this proved to be no longer true. The Prince Bishop's Minister, Baron von Fürstenberg quickly saw the implications of this experience: he had the gates thrown open and the medieval fortifications demolished. He converted the outer, earth rampart into a promenade which now encloses the whole town within a ring of lime trees.

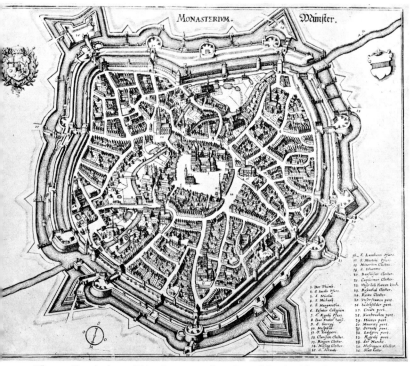

The medieval city within the protective ring of its fortifications. At the centre, the Bishop's Castle, the Cathedral Close. From Merian's plan of the town of Münster in Topographia Westphaliae

THE BUDDENTURM

All that remains of its first great fortifications dating from about 1200, is the Buddenturm. It stands at approximately the point at which the besieging soldiers forced their way into the Anabaptist town on that memorable night of the feast of St. John in the year 1535. In the course of its long history it has endured and survived many storms. We cannot know much of what may have happened within its dark and silent dungeons. Whereas originally soldiers watched over and defended the town from the tower, in later times they were imprisoned there. So they gave it the name "Rotgehäubter Satan" (Red-helmed Satan). The soldiers had an old litany which ran: "Oh Buddenturm! deliver us from your walls." The people of the town told

13

strange tales about it. Some even suspected that there was a terrible instrument of torture behind the thick walls; an "Iron Maiden" who held the condemned man in a cruel embrace of knives and daggers before hurtling the victim to a watery grave. Fortunately such a grisly tale is only the result of an inventive imagination. Today the Budden Tower has its original tiled conical roof with St. George slaying the dragon on its vane, as in former times when it was part of the fortifications.

THE PRINZIPALMARKT

The family tree of the proud merchants' houses standing on the Prinzipalmarkt dates back to the very earliest days in the history of the town. In the 12th century, when the settlement which had grown up round the Bishop's Castle was defended by a strong ring of fortifications, it was no longer necessary for the bishop to maintain fortifications round the immediate vicinity of the Cathedral, so he was able to give to the citizens narrow plots of land which were the outer half of what up to now had been the defensive moat around the bishop's castle between the Michaelistor and the Horsteberg. And right up to the present day the houses on the main market square have remained narrow. Within a short time market stalls were set up here one beside the other, and the markets gained importance as the Main Market and the Rye Market. Their greatest advantage was their closeness to the Cathedral Square where the *Send* market had originated. For the merchants in the Prinzipalmarkt had originally been traders in the *Send* market. Over the years their stalls and market-halls became the unique, arcaded gabled houses of the Prinzipalmarkt, the Roggenmarkt and Bogenstraße. In this stately row of house frontages the architectural styles of five centuries were blended to a harmonious whole. Many generations, working successively and yet in harmony, created this architectural jewel which was without equal.

The Buddenturm
Part of the early fortifications of the town, dating from about 1200

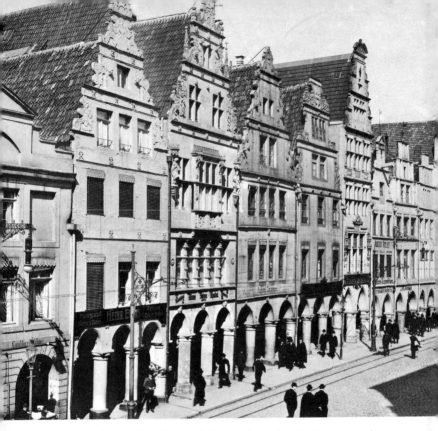

The familiar picture of the arcades and gabled houses on the
Prinzipalmarkt

The good example set in the past has had its effect even upon
the present day: although the Prinzipalmarkt fell victim to
bombing during the war, it yet rose up again with astonishing
vitality, retaining the pattern of shady arcaded walks and high
gabled frontages, but otherwise built according to present-day
techniques. The new Prinzipalmarkt cannot be expected to have
the style of the old. It took centuries to complete the old market,
a single decade to build the new.

16

The restored Prinzipalmarkt with illumination

THE "HALL-CHURCH" OF ST. LAMBERT

At the point where the Prinzipalmarkt, the Roggenmarkt and the Alter Fischmarkt (old fish-market) join, stands the dominating Town- and Market-Church of St. Lambert. In this church, "by far the most perfect example and show-piece of the late Gothic style of architecture in Westphalia" (Martin Wackernagel), the Westphalian feeling for spaciousness in hall-church building has found true expression. The Romanesque basilica with its low aisles seems to have been too confined and oppressive for the Westphalian architects. From as early as 1200 they adopted the practice of building the aisles as high as the central nave, of avoiding a spatial separation of the aisles, and of lighting the whole open space by means of large side windows. The church is conceived as a great, spacious hall. This style of building is reminiscent of the old Germanic hall and of the Westphalian farmhouse (the fourpillar construction with a spacious *Deele* or open floor). The "hall-church" was developed first in Westphalia. The church of St. Lambert is one of the finest examples of this type of construction. Entering it, the visitor is conscious of a flood of light within a great space, and experiences the intense harmony which is the secret of this style of architecture. The church was built in 1375 during the affluent Hanse era, when the middle classes had achieved prosperity and were able to build the Prinzipalmarkt. The Town Hall was built in the same century. During the French Revolution the Church of St. Lambert was a favourite refuge for French dignitaries. No fewer than sixteen bishops, archbishops and cardinals fled to Münster from France. Every Thursday a French bishop celebrated mass in the Church of St. Lambert. A famous French marshal, the Duke of Broglie who had led a campaign in Westphalia during the Seven Years War, is laid to rest before the chancel.

The Church of St. Lambert on the Prinzipalmarkt

THE TOWN HALL

In the row of high-gabled, arcaded houses on the Prinzipal-markt, the incomparable Town Hall is undoubtedly the finest example of this style of architecture. It would take a poet to sing the praises of the perfect harmony of this Gothic building. It rises effortlessly from the ground and stands with an air of confident strength, it soars upward with a restrained rhythm, bold and erect, with pilasters and stone fascias, to end in a light-hearted ornamentation of small Gothic spires decorated with sculptured figures. It is one of the noblest flowerings of Gothic architecture in Germany. We do not know exactly who created this master-piece or when it was built. But for more than six centuries its timeless perfection of form made it the most priceless jewel of the old town. Every generation has admired it. In the violent Anabaptist period it was once threatened with destruction. The worthy blacksmith Möllenhecke and his 200 supporters were fighting against the introduction of polygamy; in the struggle, he and his trusty followers being hard-pressed, retreated into the Town Hall and barricaded themselves in there. The Anabaptists set their cannon in position on the Square of St. Michael. With the barrels of the enemy guns trained threateningly on the Town Hall, Möllenhecke thought it better, before the first cannon-ball was fired, to wave his hat out of a window and surrender. By this action he did not save his life or that of his companions, but he saved the Town Hall. It also survived undamaged the Thirty Years War and other times when Münster stood in even greater peril. But in the bombing of the Second World War, with its indiscriminate destruction, it was not spared. On the afternoon of October 28th 1944 it stood in flames. As darkness fell the gable façade gave way and crashed down into the Prinzipalmarkt. But ten years later it was rebuilt to the original design of that first ingenious Gothic architect.

The re-built Town Hall and the municipal vintry

THE MESSENGER OF PEACE

The Rathaus in Münster has witnessed some events of historic importance. During the Thirty Years War Münster had the honour of offering hospitality to the Assembly of the nations of that day who hoped to bring peace to Europe. The whole of Europe was in a state of war; Westphalia's sufferings were particularly great, but in 1643 Münster was declared a town of peace, neutral and inviolable to all those engaged in war. More than a hundred ambassadors of the states which were at war, and their great entourages, travelled to Münster and Osnabrück, with all the solemnity and ceremonial of diplomatic procedure, to engage in long and complicated negotiations which were to end the "years of devastation, violence and misery" and to create an new political order in Europe. They came from many lands, from Sweden and the Netherlands, from France and Spain, from the Imperial and Papal courts, from residences of German princes and potentates who long since had been engaged in their own political activities at the expense of the Emperor. For five years they conferred and negotiated. They had come to make peace but they spent much time in dispute and contention. "Hell must be empty", wrote the ambassador of Mantua, "for all the devils are in Münster." All the world, longing for peace, turned its eyes towards Münster. At last, in May 1648, the Spanish-Dutch pact was concluded, soon to be followed by a general peace treaty. On October 25th 1648 the cannon on the ramparts, for so long silent in this war-torn age, thundered out a salute to peace. The bells of Münster and Osnabrück rang out, and an illustrated pamphlet entitled "The Postrider bringing Joy and Peace" carried these ardently awaited tidings throughout the Reich. Joy filled every heart and voices were raised in gladness. The poet joined forces with the artist and engraver. He gave the postrider the glad tidings in verse:

Neuer
Auß Münster vom 25. deß Weinmonats im Jahr
1648. abgefertigter Freud- und Friedenbringender Postreuter.

Gedruckt im Jahr nach der Geburt unsers HErrn Jesu Christi 1648.

I have come riding post-haste from Münster
And have by now covered most of my road.
I bring good news of a time of peace;
Peace has been made, all sorrow is turned away.
Mercury flies the skies and in addition Peace,
All Münster, Osnabrück and all the world rejoices,
The bells ring out and organs sweetly play,

23

Lord God we praise Thee, the joyful people sing,
Salutes thunder and roar in the air,
Flags fly bravely and everyone joins in to cheer:
Praise to God in the Highest, Peace is made,
Henceforth shall each and every one look forward to
*   better times.*
I am only sorry for the poor sword-smiths
For they have nothing to do: let swords alone,
Make out of them a plough instead, and a ploughshare too.

THE OATH OF THE AMBASSADORS

The Netherlands had particularly good reason to welcome the news of the Peace of Westphalia. Chroniclers of that time tell how on 15th May 1648 the Rathaus in Münster was adorned in festive garb. On the morning of that day the Dutch ambassadors led by Barthold van Gent and Adrian Pauw, and the Spanish

Taking the oath at the Spanish-Dutch Treaty in the Hall of Peace
Engraving after a painting by Gerard Terborch

The Arrival of the Dutch Ambassador Pauw. Painting by G. Terborch

ambassadors led by Count Peñeranda appeared at the Town Hall. They were received by the burgomasters and councillors and shown into the council chamber. On the table stood two caskets containing the peace treaties and deeds of ratification. The ambassadors made speeches in which they affirmed the consent of their king or government. Thereupon the treaty was read aloud and confirmed by oath. The Spaniards recited the words of the oath with hands laid upon a cross and the Bible. The Dutchmen took the oath by raising their hands while the words of the oath were spoken by Barthold van Gent. This solemn act was performed in public. Every chair in the council chamber was occupied. To the people of the Netherlands the events of that morning in Münster Town Hall meant even more than the achievement of a long-awaited peace treaty. After this their political independence was no longer in doubt. For eighty years they had fought against the Spanish oppressors (Goethe's play "Egmont" is set against the background of this seemingly endless struggle). Here in the Hall of Peace they had reached at last the goal for which they had striven in their War of Independence. It is easy to understand why they think of this room as a national shrine and visit it in this spirit. And how could this young nation, which has always shown such a love of art and such mastery in painting, have neglected to use as a subject for that art this important day on which its emergence was confirmed. Master Gerard Terborch came to Münster from Zwolle and recorded for posterity in a great oil painting the arrival of a Netherlands ambassador at the gates of Münster, the city of peace, and in another painting depicted the historic deed which took place in the Hall of Peace. To that nation this painting represents quite simply the conclusion of the Peace of Westphalia, although the principal treaties (between the Emperor and France and between the Emperor and Sweden) were not concluded until October, and were signed, not in the Town Hall but in the living quarters of the ambassadors.

THE HALL OF PEACE

The Peace Congress was the most important historical event to have taken place within the walls of the city of Münster. In recognition of this fact, the town decided to maintain the council chamber exactly as it was when the ambassadors of peace were active there. They even commissioned the painting of portraits of the ambassadors and their sovereigns to be hung in the council chamber. They gaze down from the walls with serious mien: Emperor Ferdinand III, King Louis XIV of France and King Philip IV of Spain and 32 ambassadors including the Papal nuncio Fabio Chigi (who later became Pope Alexander VII), the leading Imperial plenipotentiary Count von Trautmannsdorf, Count Oxenstierna of Sweden, and from the Netherlands

»The Queen of Peace«
Madonna on a chandelier in the Hall of Peace

Barthold van Gent and Adrian Pauw. The many visitors from
Germany and abroad cannot fail to be filled with awe as they
enter this memorable room, which took its name from the

The Hall of Peace, south side. At the centre the stone fireplace with a figure of Justitia and an illustration of the story of the beggar Lazarus and the rich man

nations' endeavours for peace. The great joy with which the message of peace was received is not difficult to understand, after the affliction and distress of the Thirty Years War. But not all the provisions and results of the peace treaty were welcome. Germany in particular had reason to be downcast and to view the future with mixed feelings. Imperial territory had to be abandoned and Imperial power was considerably weakened in favour of the regional princes. The first German Empire was approaching its fall. The Hall of Peace is a reminder of this too, as Levin Schücking expressed in his verses:

The Hall of Peace, north side. The room and its contents, the Judge's Table, the cupboards, panelling and portraits suffered no damage during the war

It is a gloomy, solemn place.
Many pictures gaze down with yellowed faces
Here Trautmannsdorf, there Oxenstierna –
As if they were angry at themselves

For having, in this very room, buried the splendour,
The power, the magnificence of the Empire
And concluded here a shameful peace
To the advantage of the Frenchman and in the foreigner's
tongue.

It is a gloomy, solemn place,
Through which drift shadows of dead, bygone days,
And so it pines away through the centuries,
The last refuge of ghostly thoughts.

STORIES CARVED IN WOOD

There are twenty-two document cupboards built into the main wall of the Friedenssaal which is completely lined with panelling; they run in two rows across the whole width of the wall interrupted only by the Judge's Seat. The carvings on the door-panels of the cupboards are interesting examples of late Gothic work. They date almost certainly from about 1500. Their motifs are taken from the Bible, stories of the saints, animal legends and old books of comic tales.

Reading from top left to right:

Mary Magdalene who washed the feet of Jesus, carrying in her arm a salve jar, symbol of her rôle as patron saint.

A confirmed tippler scorns the smaller drinking vessels. The artist depicts the bliss and lack of moderation of the solitary drinker who sits drinking, in the depths of a cellar until, like the writer of the drinking-song, he finishes up on his back.

The knight St. George fighting the dragon. He stands upon the monster, his sword raised ready to slay it.

Mighty Samson, a hero of the Old Testament, is seen here subduing a lion which had attacked him.

The prophet Jonas emerging after three days in the belly of the whale, a symbol of Christ's resurrection.

Two wolves holding a divided coat of arms. The crest originally painted upon it can no longer be distinguished.

A seated griffon with a blank coat of arms. Here again it is not possible to distinguish a crest.

Two men fighting, flourishing their swords. Each has been decapitated in the struggle and each is holding by the hair the same bodiless head – the head of the opponent which is at the same time his own head. A forceful representation and indictment of murderous and suicidal war.

Once again Samson, the man of strength. When the Philistines learned that he was in the town of Gaza, they lay in wait to

kill him. Then in the night he tore up an entire town gate and carried it off.

A foot-soldier carrying a broken halbard walks up to a jester who is playing the bagpipes. Can it really be a depiction of stupidity as has been suggested? Perhaps the soldier has returned from battle and is now looking for amusement and merriment. After drudgery comes revelry!

When the women of Weinsberg were permitted by the enemy to remove from the town as much as they were able to carry, they bore off their men-folk on their shoulders.

Saint Martin, a pious knight, when addressed by a beggar, tore his cloak with his sword and gave one half to the beggar.

Saint Lambert, as he is celebrating mass, is stabbed in the back by the sword of a sacrilegious robber.

A legend tells how a hind, pursued by huntsmen, sought protection and refuge with Saint Aegidius.

Saint Liudger, first bishop of Münster and like Aegidius, Lambert and Martin, a patron saint of the town, is said to have induced the tame and wild geese to cause no longer damage to the crops in the fields. (Illustration on p. 10.)

The following carving could have illustrated a story by Hans ·Sachs. A bitter quarrel between husband and wife seems to be in full swing. Could it be that the husband has left behind the last of his money, along with his authority, in the ale-house, and for this is being given a taste of the distaff by his wife?

A lion holding the divided coat of arms of the town of Münster.

The bear got more than he bargained for when he could not resist poking his nose into the sweet-smelling bee-hive: he is surprised by the lady of the house who attacks him with a heavy club.

A dog trying to run off with a bone. Here again the significance of the picture is not clear.

The messengers in the Old Teastament returning from the Promised Land where such grapes as these grow.

Monkeys imitate men and men imitate monkeys: they beat each other about the head.

These soldiers illustrate the truth that ever since Cain slew Abel, man has not been able to refrain from war and killing.

THE KING OF MÜNSTER

After the Thirty Years War, Münster was able to announce to the world the joyful tidings of peace. But a century before this Münster itself had been the scene of bloody strife when the Anabaptists acted out their violent drama there. A tailor's journeyman had come to Münster from the Netherlands and although only 25 years of age, had become the king of the Anabaptists. But the power and splendour of his reign was to be short-lived. He met his end by torture at the hands of the bishop. The reign of the Anabaptists was a sinister and inexplicable interlude in the history of Münster. The movement which spread through Upper and Lower Germany, to be extinguished in the flames of the stake, had aims deeper than simply the enforcement of its own interpretation of baptism, from which it took its name. It rejected baptism in infancy as invalid, and both preached and practised the re-baptism of adults. The movement originated in the ferment of religious and social distress of that same century which had already produced the Reformation and the Peasants' Wars; it was not satisfied with concessions and improvements, but rather rejected the whole spiritual and secular order as the work of the devil and turned its efforts to establishing the "true kingdom of the Father", the New Jerusalem as it is proclaimed in the Bible. The "golden city of Münster" was singled out to be the capital of the Kingdom of Justice. And so Anabaptists from Westphalia, Holland and Friesia came to Münster, which as a result of social and religious tensions which existed there, seemed to be a particularly favourable setting for the new Anabaptist kingdom. The prophet of the movement, Jan Matthys of Haarlem came to Münster. He strode through the streets of the town crying "Repent! Repent!" and announced that the will of the Father had been revealed to him, and that all the ungodly who refused to be baptised anew, had to be driven from the town or slain. Baptism, death or expulsion! And big crowds of whole families were driven

The King of the Anabaptists, John of Leyden, adorned with the royal insignia. Engraving by Heinrich Aldegrever

out of the town, robbed of their property. And Matthys proceeded to enforce a kind of Christian communism. Private ownership was held to be an invention of the devil. All gold and jewellery, money and provisions had to be handed over and shared. Seven deacons appointed by the prophet were in charge of its distribution. This was the stage which the Anabaptist kingdom had reached when Jan Bockelszoon of Leyden, a pupil and fellow-countryman of the prophet came to carry on the work begun by his master, and as King of the Anabaptists to carry it to its final conclusion.

THE GOLDEN CHAIN

Bishop Franz von Waldeck had given the Anabaptists sufficient time to get their position prepared in Münster. When he finally brought up his forces to besiege the town, the defences were ready for him. But the prophet Jan Matthys must really have believed his cause to be under divine protection. He had a revelation: it was the will of his Heavenly Father that he alone, accompanied only by a small group of followers should take on the bishop's besieging army. And he did not hesitate in his resolve. On Easter Day in the year 1534, he and a small band of the faithful marched out through the Ludgeri Gate to face enemy. But the Heavenly Father did not strike down the ungodly with a thunderbolt; instead a foot-soldier ran a spear through the body of the prophet. The cause of the Anabaptists would have been lost, had it not been for John of Leyden who took over their leadership. As Matthys had done before him, he continued to proclaim that the reforms which he introduced, and the orders which he issued, were revelations and visions by which the Heavenly Father made His will known to him. He had founded his kingdom in accordance with that will. It was the will of the Father that he should rule as king over all emperors, kings and princes in the world. And John furnished himself with a royal coat of arms, adorned himself with a crown, sceptre and ring, und a heavy gold chain of kingship, all of which were made from gold taken from the churches and the townspeople; he built a magnificent court about him and took

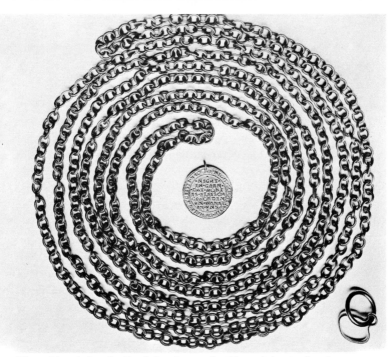

The golden chain of office belonging to the King of the Anabaptists. A gift from Bishop Franz von Waldeck to the valiant military commander and magistrate Dietrich von Merveldt zu Wolbeck

up residence, as the Prince Bishop before him, in the finest of the apartments on the Cathedral Square. He must have been a master in the skill of playing the rôle of king with dignity and conviction. Not for nothing had he, as a play-actor, always liked to be cast as a monarch. Three times each week he went in solemn procession to the market-place in front of the Town Hall where he held a public court of justice. As a token of his authority, a great sword was carried before him, the blade of which bore the words: "When I lift up this sword, I wish eternal life to the wretched sinner." It was impossible to guess in advance the outcome of the trials. It is said that John often made wise judgements. He also took pleasure in granting an unexpected pardon to those he had condemned. But more than once he is believed to have raised his sword and wished eternal life to some poor sinner.

SIXTEEN QUEENS

The sword of the Anabaptist king did not spare even one of his own queens. One day John put to the elders and preachers the question whether polygamy is not more suited to the nature of man than monogamy, and could indeed be supported by the Bible itself. The preachers had serious misgivings, particularly Rothmann, the powerful preacher and theologian, who at one time had paved the way for the teachings of the Reformation in Münster, and who had later gone over to the Anabaptists. It could not be the Father's will that lasciviousness and fornication should replace the old order. In spite of him, the prophet persisted with his plan. He argued that there were three times as many women as men living in Münster. As a result of Rothmann's preachings the nuns had deserted the convents, but there were no husbands for them. Therefore it was the will of the Father that every man should take several wives, as indeed Abraham and David and several others in the Old Testament had done. Once again on this occasion he claimed to have had a revelation from the Father, and enforced his will. For many citizens, this was the last straw. Led by the smith Möllenhecke they tried to put an end to this madness, but had to pay for their bravery with their lives. And so polygamy was established in Münster. For three days the new marriage laws were preached in the Cathedral Square. Polygamy was not merely permitted, it was obligatory. Men and women who refused were beheaded or imprisoned. John of Leyden himself chose the sixteen most beautiful young women in Münster as his wives. He is reputed to have been a handsome man much sought after by women. But before long, when starvation began to afflict the town, one of the queens rebelled against the king, saying "he feasts while the people go hungry". Then the fearful deed took place: John struck off her head with his sword and in a frenzy of blood-lust, danced round her corpse with his other wives, singing the hymn of the Baptists as they did so: "Glory be to God on high . . ."

König Johann enthaüptet sein Weib.

König Johann tantzet mit seinem Lebs Weib umb den Corper seines enthaüpten Weibes.

With his own hands, King John beheads one of his wives, Elisabeth
Wandscherer, and with his other wives dances round her corpse

¶ Ein verzeychnung der Stat Münster mit all jrer gelegenheit/mauren/thüren/
zinnen/walen/schrancken/pasteyen/vnnd geweren/wassergreben. Auch wie die
von jrem Bischoff am freytage vor Pfingsten/des M.D.xxxiiij. Jars berennt/

Contemporary drawing of the siege of the Anabaptist town

vbergeben/vnd nachmals an Sant Egidien abent an fünff orten an gelauffen/
vnd hefftig geſtürmbt worden. Alda jr ſeer vil vom Adel ſambt anderm kriegs
volck auff beiden theylen erlegen ſeind/wie etlich ſagen/bey drey tauſenden/Gott

Painted wood-cut by Eberhard Schön made in 1535

The world seemed out of joint and it was not clear how things would turn out. Meanwhile the ring of the besieging forces tightened about the city. Franz von Waldeck had succeeded in enlisting aid from neighbouring princes in Kleve and Cologne and finally at a meeting of the Reichstag in Worms, support from the Emperor too. He had tried several times to assault and storm the ramparts. Time and again his troops had been forced back with severe losses. The defences of the Anabaptists were too strong, and they were fighting with the courage of despair. But gradually the bishop was able to cut off the town completely from all outside contacts. It was no longer possible for the Anabaptists to send out their "Apostles" and their writings to Osnabrück, Warendorf, Coesfeld, Soest and further afield to Holland and Friesia to recruit aid for their cause and to demand the relief of the town. A far more grave consequence for them was that now they were no longer able to smuggle in supplies of food through the close ranks of soldiers stationed round the beleaguered town. The spectre of starvation haunted the streets and lanes bringing great misery and suffering; only the royal court escaped its visitation. Soon the people were reduced to eating cats, dogs and rats. But King John answered the complaints of his people with the sword. In June 1535, 53 citizens were executed in a single day. Then a townsman, Heinrich Gresbeck, and a foot-soldier, Hänschen von der Langenstraße stole secretly and unnoticed out of the town, determined to reveal to the bishop's troops the one weak, unguarded point in the ramparts. The besiegers accepted their word and made careful preparations for a decisive attack on the city. In Haus Coerde outside Münster the Emperor's representatives, members of the Münster town council, the commanders of the bishop's troops and the officers in charge of the mercenaries held their last council of war. Then they set to work. As soon as it was dark, on the evening of 24th June 1535, troops

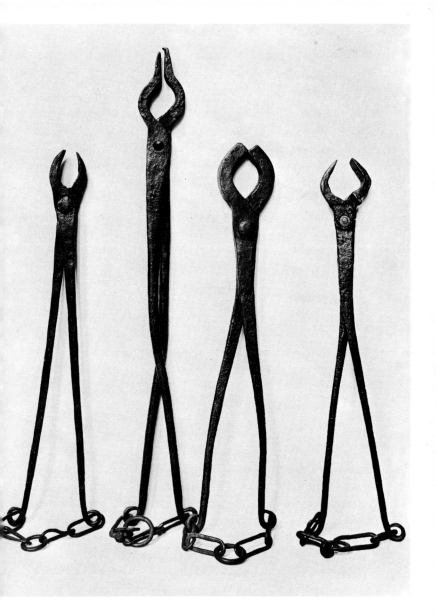

The torture irons manufactured by a Dortmund smith

and assault equipment were brought into position in front of the Kreuztor. Heinrich Gresbeck, the citizen who had betrayed the Anabaptists in order to save the town, swam across the moat; round his body he had tied a rope attached to a lightly constructed bridge which he drew across behind him. A terrible thunder storm broke over the town, just as the storming ladders were set in place and the first soldiers began to climb the rampart. They gained control of the gate and through it Wilken Steding and his soldiers invaded the town. The kingdom of the Anabaptists was destroyed amidst merciless slaughter. But the king, his executioner and governor Knipperdolling and Bernhard Krechting were taken prisoner. The bishop turned their execution into a frightful warning. He placed a high scaffold in front of the Town Hall where formerly John had sat in judgement. A crowd of avid spectators surrounded the platform. And then the executioners began their cruel work. With red-hot tongs they tortured the three Anabaptist leaders to death. Their corpses were hung on display in three cages on the tower of St. Lambert's Church.

ICONOCLASTS AND VIOLATERS OF TOWERS

Could the Aanabaptists possibly have prevented the defeat of their kingdom and their own destruction? Scarcely. Rather would their defeat have come more quickly, but that they had the ability time and again to inspire the people with a strong belief in the ultimate victory of their struggle and with a renewal of faith in the Anabaptist cause. When John of Leyden took over the leadership of the beleaguered town, the outcome of the campaign was already decided. So it is all the more surprising to consider what the Anabaptists were able to achieve under his leadership, and the way in which time and again he was able to hold them together right up to the bitter end. He saw the importance of both outward and inward strength, of powerful defences manned by defenders with strong convictions. Years later,

The cages hanging on the tower of the Church of St. Lambert, in which the bodies of the Anabaptist leaders were placed

military experts still admired the layout of the town's fortifications, and John was well aware of his achievement. When he was in prison, the bishop reproached him for having spoiled the town, but he replied proudly that, on the contrary, he had delivered up to him an impregnable town. In constructing the fortifications and ramparts he used both stonework from the churches, which he called stone-pits, and valuable sculptures, and thus recklessly and irretrievably destroyed many masterpieces of Westphalian art. In 1898 Max Geisberg made diggings near the Kreuztor in search of the sculptures and brought to light some interesting finds. All books (with the exception of the Old and New Testament) had been confiscated and were burnt to ashes in the Cathedral Square.

Many unique manuscripts and printed books from the time of the Brothers of the Common Life and the Humanists must have been destroyed in the fires. But that was not the end of it. The cloth-merchant and executioner Knipperdolling made his own interpretation of a phrase in the Bible "the exalted shall be abased and the humble shall be exalted". The full meaning of it had, he claimed, been revealed to him by God. The towers of six churches were to be removed. And Knipperdolling did not delay in setting his men to work. The roof-trusses of the towers were sawn through and the whole upper section was sent crashing to the ground. Both the Cathedral and the Church of Our Lady (Überwasser Kirche) were "abased" in this way. Perhaps the Anabaptists in the town believed at first in this interpretation of the Bible according to Knipperdolling, but the besiegers outside the walls were at a loss to understand what was happening when they saw the towers of the churches crashing to the ground amidst great clouds of dust. Later their suspicions were confirmed. Cannon had been set in position on the towers from which vantage-point they were able to fire with deadly accuracy on the forces of the bishop encamped below. But even such wiles and stratagems of war could not prevent the ultimate defeat of the Anabaptists.

The tower of the Church of Our Lady (Überwasserkirche), one of the
most massive church towers in Westphalia, used by the Anabaptists
as a cannon emplacement

The Zwinger standing where the River Aa flows out of the old part of the town. Its cone-shaped roof slopes outwards to the exterior walls and inwards to the central court

THE ZWINGER

Hardly had the echoes of the Anabaptist disturbances died away and the town come once again under the episcopal yoke of the Prince Bishop, when Franz von Waldeck decided it was advisable to set up reliable strong-points within the town. By the spring of 1536 he had laid the foundation stone of a powerful keep, the Zwinger, which was to be built at the point where the river Aa flows out of the town. A garrison of the bishop's troops was stationed in this sturdy bastion. Of other events which took place there, we only know in part. There is no lack of sensational stories. One obvious use for it was as a prison, and at one time there was a treadmill in it for drawing water; at another time it housed a gun-powder mill, and one day there was an explosion and the roof was burnt off. It is even said that a gallows once stood in the central courtyard, on which deserters from the army were put to death. When the fortifications were dismantled in 1765, the Zwinger was left standing, probably on account of its great strength (its walls are nearly 7 foot thick). But it served no useful purpose until an artist had the idea of turning it into a centre for artists. Then it was taken over by youth groups who filled it with singing and dancing, until, during the war, bombs reduced even this massive bulwark to ruins.

THE ANNUNCIATION

Just how little the vitality of Münster suffered in the spiritual confusion and physical sufferings of the Anabaptist era was made clear in a remarkable way during the decades which followed. It was as if creative forces had been dammed up and had to break through at last. The Council Chamber which in the following century was to serve as the meeting place of the great Peace Congress was enriched by fine carving and panelling-work, as was the Chapter House of the Cathedral. The Kramer-amtshaus and the Heeremansche Hof belong to this period, as well as other Renaissance buildings which have not survived. In the west portal of the Cathedral the sculptures of the Wise and Foolish Virgins were set up. The magnificent Salvator gable was added to the east transept. The astronomical clock which had been destroyed by the Anabaptists was renovated and given the form in which we see it today. The most outstanding and versatile artist of the second half of the 16th century was Hermann tom Ring, whose signature may also be recognised in many a building. He is among the greatest masters of the Westphalian school of painting, and his *Annunciation* must count as a masterpiece not only of Westphalian but also of western art as a whole. From this altar painting we can also learn much about Münster's social history. The middle-class citizens of Münster in the Renaissance age must have lived in surroundings

The Annunciation. Altar-panel painting by Hermann tom Ring from the Church of Our Lady. Today housed in the Westphalian Museum

very similar to those of this fair-haired Mary depicted here in a comfortable, well-furnished room as she receives the message of the angel.

THE KNIGHT IN THE "PARADIES"

Even though an extraordinary degree of misfortune seems to have marked the fate of many works of sculpture in Münster, enough examples remain – in spite of Anabaptist uprisings and bombing raids – to give proof of the high qualtiy of the sculpture which was created here. Outstanding examples are the splendid statues of Apostles, founders and patrons which stand, austere and grave, in the *Paradies* or vestibule of the Cathedral. They are among the finest achievements of medieval sculpture. The art historian Johannes Klein considers the statues in Münster Cathedral to be "some of the finest examples of German art of the 13th century". The Paradies is built as a vestibule in front of the west transept of the Cathedral. Originally it opened on to the Cathedral Square through three large arches. The side walls too, against each of which two statues now stand, were open arcades. The vestibule was enclosed when the front half of the present building was added and a second floor was built over it to house the Cathedral library. So the statues withdrew into a shadowy half-light. Entering the Paradies, the visitor senses that this hall is something more than an ordinary vestibule. He can sense the living presence of a great, timeless art. This hall houses "the most comprehensive work of the whole of western German monumental sculpture" (P. Clemen). Along the main wall, arranged symmetrically to the right and left of the entrance to the Cathedral, stand the figures of the Apostles, above life-size, full of majesty and severe dignity. For the most part they escaped the destructive fury of the Anabaptists. But two Apostles, and in particular the central figure of St. Paul, patron saint of the Cathedral, fell victim to them. The figures of the Apostles are the work of several sculptors of the late Romanesque period. The fine examples of early Gothic sculpture along the side walls belong to a rather later date, about 1260; those on the right represent St. Laurence and Bishop Dietrich von Isenburg, those on the left St. Mary Magdalene

The *Paradies*
The vestibule leading to the west transept of the cathedral

The Knight in the vestibule of the cathedral (the Paradies)

and a knight whose identity is uncertain. But no matter who the individual portrayed here may have been, this figure epitomises the ideal of knighthood. Until recently only a small circle of discerning connoisseurs recognised and appreciated the importance of the knight and indeed of the whole collection of venerable stone figures, which must rank as artistic masterpieces. Here in the shadows of the *Paradieshalle* is a unique treasure which can rival the famous sculptures in the Cathedrals of Naumburg or of Bamberg.

MÜNSTERLANDERS SEEN BY A SCULPTOR

Another master of the later period is known to us by name; he is Henrick Brabender-Beldensnyder. The group of spectators at Christ's entry into Jerusalem is an example of his work. In 1516 he created these life-sized figures for the west gable of the Cathedral. It was probably their inaccessible position high above the western entrance which saved them from the iconoclastic attacks of the Anabaptists. Since then they have been brought down and placed in the Cathedral cloisters, to save them from further damage by wind and weather. (Since the west side of the building has been closed, the statues of the Wise and Foolish Virgins have also been removed from their original position at the western entrance.) As an exponent of late Gothic expressionism, Henrick Brabender-Beldensnyder depicted the people of his own native region. These spectators at the roadside, watching as the Son of David arrives in the name of the Lord, are peasants from the Münster region. They have opened their mouths to cry out "Hosanna", but even before it has reached their lips, the joyful cry seems to have been transformed into an expression of disconcerted amazement, even of anxious fright. Is it possible that what they see before them can really be happening? The figures of the two old men who are in the act of spreading out their cloaks before Jesus, express an extraordinary degree of movement while yet retaining an attitude of moderation and reserve. The restrained gestures reveal a deep excitement and genuine emotion, which suffuse the entire figures. Something of intense significance is happening before their eyes and in their souls. Such art is both a masterly depiction of human character and at the same time genuine native art, in

Group of spectators at Christ's entry into Jerusalem. Sculpture by Henrik Brabender-Beldensnyder for the west gable of the cathedral. Today it stands in the cloisters

which the artist convincingly depicts people of his own homeland both in their external appearance and their qualities of character.

Aerial view of the town centre, the old Cathedral Close. In the foreground: the Church of St. Lambert, the Prinzipalmarkt an the Town Hall.
——▶

THE CATHEDRAL

Within its ancient ramparts Münster cherishes a rich and valuable architectural heritage, in which it is still possible to recognise those forces which have determined the development of the town. There are three forces which, over the centuries have successively and simultaneously shaped the form and face of Münster: they are the church, the middle classes and the nobility. It was they who built the churches and the ecclesiastical residences, the Prinzipalmarkt and other fine, burghers' houses, and the mansions of the nobility including the *Erbdrostenhof*. But the most outstanding achievements of these three forces, which have given Münster its characteristic appearance, are the Cathedral, the Town Hall and the Palace. The Cathedral of St. Paul situated on the *Horsteberg* is the most massive and dignified building in Münster, it is the third one, built from 1225 to 1264, (while the first one dates back to the times of St. Liudger in the 9th century). In the history of architecture, the Cathedral is a unique example of monumental building at the time of the transition from Romanesque to Gothic style. The triple-naved main body of the church built in the style of the basilica, widens into two transepts. Soaring arches above massive corner pillars curve upwards to achieve the impressive feeling of spaciousness of this Westphalian church. Throughout the centuries much has been altered and much added, so that now the church, with its adjoining chapels and entrances richly ornamented with sculptures, stands as a massive and outstandingly attractive complex, an incomparable example of native Westphalian art. "The cathedral in Münster is not only the largest in area of the Westphalian episcopal churches but also artistically the most important. The architectural form of its interior is the most impressive of any church throughout Westphalia. Here we have a creation which can only be called sublime. The artistic skill of many generations has contributed to create this masterpiece. The dedication of a town and people to art is expressed for all time in this buil-

ding" (Werner Burmeister). In the Second World War, the
cathedral was badly damaged. Inexplicably, it was bombed
many times, as if it were a military stronghold. As well as the

fabric of the building, towers, portals, pillars and arches, its wealth of ornamental sculpture was also largely destroyed. Reconstruction was completed within a decade. The restoration of no other building aroused such keen interest among the citizens as that of the cathedral. In lively discussions every aspect was considered. The west wing of the building containing the great Gothic entrance with figures of the Wise and Foolish Virgins, dating from 1592, was closed. Instead of the earlier tracery window, or the even earlier rose window, it was given sixteen small circular windows, popularly nicknamed the "Seelenbrause" (Holy watering-can). Considerable and well-deserved admiration has been expressed for the newly-designed interior. The Cathedral of Münster is more beautiful and splendid than ever before.

THE CARDINAL

At the very time when the great Cathedral of St. Paul was reduced to ruins, the bishop of this church rose to fame as a figure of historic greatness. It was here that Clemens August Count von Galen, a true knight *sans peur et sans reproche*, carried on his battle for the word of God and the rights of man, within the national socialist state. His sermons preached against tyranny met with a world-wide response. It must have been clear to him that they would bring him imprisonment and death rather than renown. Yet he was prepared to stake his life with courage and with scorn for every danger, and overnight he became known as the "Lion of Münster". When, after his period of probation he returned to his bishopric from Rome, now wearing the Cardinal's purple, he was met in a triumphal reception by the townspeople, which was soon to culminate in a dramatic finale. He died on March 22nd. 1946. The historic rôle which he had been called to play was over. The scenes which concluded his earthly life could not fail to stir the emotion and win the admiration of even the greatest dramatic poet. The bishop lives

on in the memory of his people as the symbol of Westphalian steadfastness, as a courageous fighter who went his way unafraid, faithful to the motto emblazoned on his coat of arms: nec laudibus nec timore. Neither praise nor fear could turn him from his path. He was laid to rest in one of the chapels of the Galen family which had been built in 1663, in the ambulatory

The Cardinal's tomb in front of the Ludgerus altar in the great cathedral

of the choir, by Christoph Bernhard von Galen, a bishop of the same family. Here in three chapels are the tombs of three bishops from this noble family; in the first, the suffragan Bishop Maximilian Gereon von Galen, in the second, Cardinal von Galen and in the third, Prince Bishop Christoph Bernhard von Galen.

THE ASTRONOMICAL CLOCK

In the cathedral, on the wall of the choir ambulatory, there is a cleverly constructed astronomical clock which has survived the war unharmed. Like the clock in Strassburg Cathedral, its own legend has grown up round it. The story tells how, by decree of the Town Council, the master craftsman who had constructed the clock was to have his eyes struck out, lest he should ever create a similar masterpiece for another town. The master begged to be allowed to see his work for the last time. Then with a single movement he brought his mysterious creation to a halt. Since that time no one had been able to set it going again. This legend may have arisen at a period during which the clock had been stopped for a long time, and so had achieved the reputation of having a secret mechanism which only the master understood. But after it was repaired and was working like any other clock, it enjoyed such great popularity that on one occasion the Cathedral Chapter itself took exception to it because "during mass and vespers, a hitherto unprecedented tumult and insolent disturbance could be heard from the spectators and rabble who had come to watch the Procession of the Three Kings". This could not be allowed to continue. The first clock was destroyed by the Anabaptists. There is no reliable record of its age at that time. Immediately after the Anabaptist era, work was begun on a new clock to be hung in the same position. Science, craftsmanship and art worked together to produce this masterpiece. The work was carried out by the mathematician and printer Dietrich Tzwyvel (the owner of the firm which later became the Regensberg Press); Johann von Aachen, a Franciscan monk, cathedral preacher and almanac maker; and the smith Nikolaus Windemaker. But it was not only the astronomical knowledge and technical skill of the late Middle Ages which contributed to the elaborate construction of this much-admired clock, the mechanism of which is driven by massive weights. A sculptor and a painter were also called in to ensure

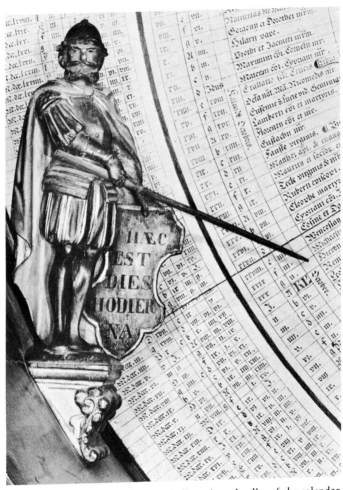

Throughout the year, each day is indicated on the disc of the calendar

the artistic merit of the clock's outward form. The wooden
figures of the Madonna and Child, the Three Kings, the man
carrying a watchman's horn, and his wife are the work of Johann

The astronomical clock: at the top the Procession of the Three Kings,
in the middle the clock with a map of the world, the zodiac and the
planets, and below, the Calendarium

Brabender-Beldensnyder. The splendid architectural background and the groups of spectators at the procession of the Three Kings, which decorate the upper part and direct attention towards its centre, were painted by Ludger tom Ring the Elder.

THE PROCESSION OF THE THREE KINGS

The Procession of the Three Kings and the Glockenspiel provide a most original variation on the usual, humdrum way of measuring and marking the passage of time, and have made the astronomical clock a popular attraction. On either side of the upper part there stand two carved figures; on the far left, the watchman (the Tutemännchen) who marks the full hour with a note on his horn, while his wife accompanies each note of the horn by striking a bell with a hammer; to the right Chronos carrying an hour-glass and scythe which he holds out to Death, who strikes the quarter-hours with a hammer. His foot is set inexorably on the earth's globe. At 12 o'clock midday the clock springs to life. Hardly has the twelfth stroke of the hour died away when a door to the right of the centre opens, and the Three Kings make their appearance, pass with slow, measured steps in procession, bowing gracefully before the Madonna and Child, to disappear on the other side. The procession is accompanied by the glockenspiel playing an old Christmas song. The melody dies away and only the steady ticking of the clock remains. There is much in this curious work of art to puzzle the observer. A thousand questions could be posed. It requires a considerable, specialised knowledge to understand everything which is expressed here in astronomical terms about the sun, moon and stars, about the zodiac and the fixed firmament, about Mars and Venus, Mercury and Saturn. A curious feature of the clock in the centre is that its huge hand moves in reverse, starting the day at midnight at the bottom of the clock face. The Calendarium with a picture for each month of the year is particularly interesting.

The Procession of the Three Kings on the astronomical clock

The calendar disc on the astronomical clock with the illustrations of the months of the year. In the middle, St. Paul, the patron saint of the cathedral

January loves revels,
  and eating
and drinking
  by the fire.

Pocula Janus amat
  comeditque et potat ad ignem.

Then chilly February
  covers over
the rivers
  with frost.

Contrahit inde gelu
  fluvios Februarius algens.

Then March
  prunes the trees and vines
and breaks up the
  ploughed fields.

Deinde putat vites
  et scindit Martius arva.

April opens
   up the ground
and brings
   forth flowers.

Aprilis terras
   aperit, cum florida prodit.

In May
   the dewy edges
of the verdant glades
   are tinder of love.

Ros et frons nemorum
   Majo sunt fomes amoris.

June shears
   our sheep
here as
   they play.

Tondet oves nostras
   hinc Junius ille ludentes.

July brings
a harvest
of good hay for
our cattle.

*Fena metit pecori
nostrati Julius alma.*

And August
stacks the
cut corn in
the fields.

*Augustusque spicas
demessas cogit in agris.*

September entrusts
the seeds
to the ploughed
furrows.

*Semina committit ·
sulcis September aratis.*

Thereafter
October gathers in
the ripened
grapes.

Post hec Oktober
coctas bene colligit uvas.

November
delights everyone
in slaughtering
the pigs.

Laetatur porcos
mactando quisque November.

December splits
the firewood
for the hearths,
plundering the thickets.

Ligna focis findit
spolians virgulta Dezember.

THE CALENDARIUM ON THE CATHEDRAL CLOCK

At ground level, below the astronomical clock, the calendarium is kept in a recessed circular niche, behind a hand-wrought protective grid. Its broad disc is divided into three circles. The outer circle contains a complete almanac for 532 years, from the year of the cathedral's completion in 1540 up to the year 2071. The inner ring registers all the days of one year. Here we are able to read off the day, month and year in which we are now living. The Saints' Days are listed too. At the middle of the disc the astronomer has been replaced by the artist. The painter has been given a free hand, and in twelve charming miniature paintings he depicts scenes throughout the course of a year. The artist is unknown. He may have been one of the Brunswick school of monogrammists, a Netherlander or even a member of the gifted tom Ring family. They are pictures from the life of the people, or, more exactly, from the life of a medieval town in which the rhythm is determined by the changing seasons. Each of the twelve pictures is accompanied by a Latin verse.

THE BISHOP OF THE CANNON

The old episcopal town stood for a long time under the worldly domination of the bishop's crosier. These princes of the church not only prayed and saved souls but they also waged wars, one of them indeed on such a scale that he earned for himself the nicknames "Bombenbernhard" and the "Bishop of the Cannon". Christoph Bernhard von Galen who came to power immediately after the Thirty Years War, was involved in military campaigns throughout Europe. He waged virtually continuous war against Holland. The French "roi soleil" was sometimes his ally, sometimes his opponent, as were too the Emperor and the Great Elector. He supported the Emperor in the Turkish War of 1663/64, but was later accused by the Emperor of high treason, so Christoph Bernhard ordered that the Emperor's representa-

CHRISTOF. BERNART,
Biffchop *van* Munfter. &.

Prince Bishop Christoph Bernhard von Galen (1650–1678)
Engraving by an unknown master

tive who had been sent to arrest him should be beheaded and quartered. The gesture of a truly Machiavellian prince of the church. He succeeded in taking his place among the great powers of his day. Louis XIV of France, on his own admission, feared only him and the Great Elector amongst all the German princes; the Great Elector visited him frequently in Sassenberg and Beckum. And yet he did not succeed in founding a viable state. So Münster bore the brunt of his political activities. Several times Christoph Bernhard conquered the old Hanse town which, on the basis of its privileged position during the peace negotiations, was fighting for the status of a Free Town of the Reich, and he deprived it of all its liberties. Christoph Bernhard expressed his scorn for the limited potentialities of the common people when he put up a notice on the house of the United Guilds which read "Cobbler, stick to your last". Münster turned in vain for help to the Hanse and to Holland. The great days of bourgeois power were over. The age of absolutism had arrived and the bourgeois world and bourgeois culture hat to yield to a new courtly hierarchy. The citizens of Münster have not forgiven Christoph Bernhard for his power politics. And yet Christoph Bernhard von Galen was the most important prince of the church in his century and one of the greatest bishops of Münster, who lived his life fearlessly as a baroque autocrat, but who also contributed much to the renewal of religious life after the great war.

THE MANSIONS OF THE NOBILITY

The visitor exploring the streets of the town (before the bombing raids of the Second World War), must frequently have stopped in surprise before a wrought-iron gate through which he could see a distinguished mansion standing a little withdrawn from the road. Projecting side wings enclosed an open courtyard, the Court of Honour, beyond which lay the main building. An open flight of steps led up to it. The richly decorated central façade was surmounted by a fine triangular pediment, proudly bearing the coat of arms of a noble family as the distinguishing mark of the house. The town dwellings of the Münster nobility presented just such a picture. In Münster, the mansions of the nobility are the urban equivalent of the moated castles in

The Heeremansche Hof on Königsstraße

the country, where the nobleman and his family spent the summer. But for use during the winter, or whenever he wanted to be in the residence town, which was the political and cultural centre of the region, he built himself a fine town mansion. Most date from about 1700 and are built in the Baroque style in red

The Erbdrostenhof, most beautiful and magnificent of the mansions
of the nobility

brick with window-frames in light coloured dressed stone. The
leading architects of the day (Pictorius, Schlaun, Lipper) were
commissioned to build these mansions. They do not all conform
to the style described here, which was that of the heyday of the
wealthy nobility. Many, like the Heeremansche Hof on König-

strasse and the Romberger Hof, built in the classical style and now destroyed, were set forward on the line of the street. It is regrettable that such a tragically large number of these mansions of the nobility fell victim to bombing during the war. No single one of them survived the war unscathed, and it was possible to restore only a very few to their previous architectural splendour. The Heeremansche Hof, a fine Renaissance building, later housed the Supreme Court of Law of North Rhine-Westphalia. The most splendid of all the mansions is the Erbdrostenhof, a palatial edifice of great nobility built by the brilliant architect Johann Conrad Schlaun on a corner site on Salzstrasse. The Erbdrostenhof is the finest example of the aristocratic architecture which flourished in Münster and which was fittingly crowned by the building of the Prince Bishop's Palace.

THE PALACE RESIDENCE

As the seat of a Prince Bishop, Münster had long been a residence town, but it was not until the splendour of the Prince Bishops began to decline that the stately Palace Residence was built. It is true that several Prince Bishops had, before election, pledged themselves to build a permanent residence. But the first one to go ahead with the plan was the Elector Maximilian Friedrich and his capable Minister von Fürstenberg. The result was a palace residence which, in the grandeur of its plan and the perfection of its Rococo-Baroque form, can rival any other residence in the whole of northern Germany. The palace and its spacious grounds made up of gardens and a fore-court was a late work of the great architect Johann Conrad Schlaun. In 1787, the building and its interior decoration were completed and it was ready to receive as its first occupant the ruling Prince Bishop of Münster, the Elector of Cologne and Grand Master of the Teutonic Order, Maximilian Franz. He was the youngest son of the Empress Maria Theresia. But in Münster the two sworn enemies of the 18th century within Germany met in con-

Residenz Schloß des Kurfürsten von Köllen als
Fürst-Bischoffs zu Münster außerhalb der Stadt
Münster.

Vuë de la nouvaux Chateaux de Munster du Cotte de
Ville erige de Sa. A. E. El. de Cologne Prince et Evequ
de Munster

Se vend à Augsbourg au Negoce comun de l'Academie Imperiale d'Empire des Arts liberaux avec Privilege de Sa Majeste Imperiale et avec Defense de donner ni de vendre les Copies.

General view of the electoral palace built in the Rococo style. The
supraporte

flict, and here too Prussia triumphed over the House of Habs-
burg. Instead of Habsburgs, the first inhabitants of the palace
were General von Blücher and Baron vom Stein, who as representatives of Prussian authority brought Münster under Prussian administration. Before long Napoleon's princes and gene-
rals took over the palace and received the homage of the old
court nobility, until the Prussians returned once more. They
made Münster the capital of the newly founded province of
Westphalia (1815). From that time onwards the palace served
as the quarters of the Lord Lieutenant of the province and of the
General Officer Commanding. After being completely gutted by
fire in the last war, it was put to a different use, and was restored as the University's main building.

79

FROM THE CHRONICLES OF THE UNIVERSITY

The history of the University of Münster includes the curious fact that the University was founded twice. No less curious is the fact that it has a pre-history which extends over a longer period than does its actual history. Towards the end of the Middle Ages the town of Münster entered a period of intellectual activity which might have been expected to culminate in the founding of a university. This was during the decades around 1500, when the humanists and the Brothers of the Common Life elevated the spiritual life of the affluent and esteemed Hanse town to admirable heights. And yet the famous Cathedral School in which great scholars were active and which produced great scholars, still did not become a university. Instead King John of Leyden founded his kingdom of the Anabaptists which despised all scholarship. When, after the fall of the Anabaptists, a further hundred years had come and gone, the time once again seemed ripe. In 1629 and 1631 the Pope and the Emperor had granted the privilege of foundation, and the states of the province had accorded the not inconsiderable sum of 20,000 thalers for the foundation of a university, but once again history was to intervene to prevent it. The Thirty Years War turned people's minds to other matters and placed Münster, as the setting for the Peace Congress, at the centre of political activity in Europe. Twenty years after the war, when the energetic provincial governor Christoph Bernhard von Galen once again took up the old plan, it seemed that now, at last, the university would indeed be founded. Christoph Bernhard himself believed that the realization of the plan was imminent. He estimated the exact cost of establishing a university with four faculties, and with his own hand he had already drafted a programme for a five-day-long celebration of the university's foundation and for a foundation banquet of Baroque richness and abundance. Who would not have been a willing guest when he reads of the fine fare Christoph Bernhard intended to serve: 20 calves, 20

Formerly the residence of the Prince Bishop, today the university
Built between 1767–1773 by Schlaun

stags, 30 roe-deer, 15 wild boars, 150 hares, 500 partridges, 75 large turkeys, 150 small turkeys, 200 capon, 250 pigeons, 500 quail, 500 large carp, 1000 tench and in addition Rhine salmon and crabs, wheaten bread from Meppen and beer from Sassenberg, Paderborn, Hamm, Wolbeck and Minden. The banquet had only one flaw: it did not take place. The university was not founded. Once again the God of War ruled the day. Campaigns and cannon devoured so much money that there was none left over for calves, crabs and capon. A further hundred years had to come and go before the plan was taken up again by the right man.

FÜRSTENBERG'S FOUNDATION

Franz von Fürstenberg came from Schloss Herdringen in Sauerland in the duchy of Westphalia. He became Münster's greatest statesman. As Minister and permanent representative of the Elector of Cologne in the Prince Bishopric of Münster he had a proud record of distinguished services to the town which included the founding of the University of Münster. It was intended primarily as a regional university. Fürstenberg went so far as to seek out gifted young local men whom he educated for a university career and then appointed to teach in his university. In spite of this self-imposed limitation, Fürstenberg was able to assemble a body of teachers who were men of considerable standing. This young university, founded in 1773 although not opened until 1780, showed great promise, and yet fate was not to continue long to smile upon it. In 1802, after Napoleon had disturbed the political relationships in Europe, Münster allied herself first with Prussia, then later with France and then once more with Prussia. Baron vom Stein drew up ambitious plans for the extension of Fürstenberg's foundation. Had his plan been realised, Münster would have possessed the most up-to-date university throughout the whole of Germany at that time. But it was not to be. In 1818 Münster University was closed in

The entrance to the old university in the former Jesuit college (1615).
The building was destroyed in the war

favour of the newly-founded University of Bonn. This was in fulfilment of a promise the king had made to the Rhinelanders who had also thrown in their lot with Prussia. The just claims of Münster were disregarded. But the Westphalians did not accept such treatment without protest. On the contrary, there followed a bitter struggle for the re-founding of the University of Münster, and a politician coined the phrase which was to become a familiar saying "Bonn's reins are made of Münster leather". All that remained in Münster of Fürstenberg's foundation was a college which was later turned into an Academy of Theology and Philosophy. It is quite likely that the matter would have rested there, had not a Westphalian member of the Prussian Upper House, Prince Otto zu Salm-Horstemar (popularly nick-named "Handsome Otto") won over his friend Emperor William II to support the cause of Münster University. On July 1st 1902 His Imperial Majesty gave royal assent to the establishment of a Faculty of Law and Political Science and at the same time to the elevation of the Academy to the status of a university. This was the second founding of the University of Münster which was later called the Westphälische Wilhelms-Universität after its Imperial founder. In 1914 a Protestant Faculty of Theology and in 1925 a Faculty of Medicine were added. Today, after the reconstruction of almost all the buildings and institutes which were destroyed during the war, it is one of the largest, most important and most beautiful universities in Germany.

FAMILIA SACRA

The citizens of Münster did not really enjoy the absolute rule of the Prince-Bishops, and only later did they come to realise how much that period had contributed to the physical and spiritual development of Münster. Although the Elector of Cologne, as Prince Bishop of Münster did not hold court there, the town was nevertheless an important focus and centre of influence. But it was not the courtly culture of the enlightened Rococo age which unexpectedly came to flower in Münster in the second half of the 18th century, but an entirely individual, spiritual movement peculiar to Münster. Never since the days of the humanist Ru-

The Münster circle. Painting by Theobald von Oer

From left to right: Franz Kaspar *Buchholtz*, a Welbergen landowner –
Dr. Franz Ferdinand von *Druffel*, physician – Georg *Kellermann*,
tutor to the young Count Stolberg (he died in 1847 as bishop elect
before his consecration) – two sons of Count Stolberg – Countess
Stolberg – Count *Stolberg* – Erbdroste Adolf von *Droste Vischering* –
Vicar general and minister (retired) Franz von *Fürstenberg* – Amalie
Princess von *Gallitzin* – Bernard *Overberg*, »teacher of teachers« and
regent of the priests' seminary – Franz Otto Freiherr von *Droste-
Vischering*, canon – Clemens August Freiherr von *Droste-Vischering*,
later Archbishop of Cologne – Marianne, daughter of the princess –
Caspar Max Freiherr von *Droste-Vischering*, suffragan bishop, later
Bishop of Münster – Prof. *Kistemaker*, headmaster of the Paulinum –
Anton Matthias *Sprickmann*, writer and professor of law – Theodor
Katerkamp, professor of ecclesiastical history – in the background, the
princess's son, Prince Demetrius von Gallitzin, a missionary to North
America who later became Vicar General in Philadelphia.

dolf von Langen and the monk Johannes Veghe had Münster experienced a spiritual upsurge of such vigour. Once again Franz von Fürstenberg was the man who inspired and led this spiritual re-birth. Together with the poet and professor of law Sprickmann and the theologian and educationalist Overberg, he introduced and carried out a sweeping programme of educational reform and raised the ideal of Christian education and humanity to such heights that the fame of his teachings spread far across the land. Important figures of the day, who took their education and Christianity seriously, made their way to Münster. The Dutch Platonist philosopher Hemsterhuis read Fürstenberg's educational programme and gave it to Princess Amalie von Gallitzin to read; as a result, instead of going to the Lake of Geneva, they both travelled to Münster. Goethe's friend Friedrich Leopold Count von Stolberg came and stayed. Others who became part of this circle included Klopstock and Matthias Claudius, the editor of the newspaper the *Wandsbecker Bote*. And even Goethe, returning in 1792 from his "Campaign in France", brought his coach by way of Münster so that he could visit Amalie von Gallitzin and Fürstenberg, and spend a few days in the princess's house in *Grüne Gasse* in this "pious, virtuous company". And so Weimar and Münster met, not in agreement but in mutual respect. Each one remained firm in his conviction. It was not the spirit of Weimar classicism which had seized hold of Münster, but the spirit of the Christian way of life, Christian humanity and Christian charity. The Münster group has been aptly named *familia sacra*, the holy family.

AMALIE VON GALLITZIN

Amalie von Gallitzin increasingly took over the rôle of the mother of this family. This remarkable woman came from the world of high society. Her path led from Berlin by way of the Hague to Münster and Angelmodde. She was born in Berlin on 28th August 1748, daughter of the Prussian Field Marshal von

Amalie von Gallitzin · Painting by Franz Hemsterhuis

Schmettau; she was lady-in-waiting to Princess Ferdinand of
Prussia, and at twenty years of age married the Russian Prince
Dimitri von Gallitzin who was living in the Hague as ambassa-
dor to the Czar. But life at court with its diplomatic receptions

and social gatherings seemed, to this beautiful woman endowed with every gift of nature and intellect, to be hollow and empty. Influenced by the French encyclopedist Diderot and the Dutch philosopher Hemsterhuis, she turned to the study of ancient languages, mathematics and philosophy; she withdrew to a small farm near the Hague, laid aside hooped petticoats, tight lacing and such modish conceits and devoted herself wholly to striving for philosophical understanding, to her spiritual development and to the education of her children. Then she heard reports of the new spiritual life which was flourishing in Münster. She made her way there and became an important member of Fürstenberg and Overberg's little community, continuing along the spiritual path she had chosen in unswerving confidence to the final point at which she rejected completely the teachings of the Age of Enlightenment and gave herself over entirely to Christianity. When together with Fürstenberg and Hemsterhuis, she first visited Goethe in Weimar, the poet did not approve of her "discarding the costume of the age, and wanting, as a woman, to put aside her womanliness". But it was not long before he was admitting that "the Princess is the sort of person it is quite impossible to imagine before you have met her. An exquisite soul". Hamann probably summed up her character most aptly when he wrote that she "languished with passion for greatness and profoundness of heart". "The Princess is truly a paragon of a woman." She believed the supreme law of the Christian faith to be love of God and of one's fellow men, and she lived by this belief with her whole heart and soul. She died in Münster on 27th April 1806. Her last wish was fulfilled. "I would like to be buried in that part of the churchyard in Angelmodde where the poor are buried."

THE MAGUS OF THE NORTH

There was probably no one at that time who felt himself more strongly drawn to Münster than the "Magus of the North", the Königsberg philosopher Johann Georg Hamann. Friedrich Karl von Moser in Darmstadt read Hamann's publication "Magi of the East in Bethlehem" and afterwards wrote "The simple letter of a German lay brother to the Magus of the North" in which he aligned himself with Hamann against unbelieving Rationalist critics of the Bible. "Let others pursue their will-o'-the-wisp heresies, you have seen His star, you are the Magus of the North." And so Moser gave the name to Hamann by which he was to be known in history, the Magus of the North, who had seen and followed the star of Bethlehem. But the philosopher was just then eking out a scanty living in Königsberg, constantly hard-pressed to provide for his own and his children's needs. Then letters of admiration and respect began to arrive unexpectedly from Münster. Franz Kaspar Bucholtz of Welbergen asked to be accepted as Hamann's spiritual son; he proved himself a generous patron by giving the philosopher 4,000 thalers to allay his financial difficulties and by inviting him to Münster. When Hamann learned that the Princess Gallitzin was very interested in him too, he asked in astonishment "How is it that Minerva has come to trouble herself about Till Eulenspiegel?" But he was happy to accept the invitation from far-off Westphalia, for he felt that in Münster he would be completely understood. Münster had called him and he came buoyed up by the hope that here he would find people of his own kind. "Not Weimar but Münster is the hearth at which I hope to find courage and renewed youth." A description of his first view of the town by night betrays his own exalted emotions and high hopes: "The very streets seemed to me like halls of a great temple brilliantly lit from an altar." And Hamann was not disappointed. The Catholic princess revered this Protestant Socrates as if he were a saint: "I feel more and more strongly convinced that

The grave of the philosopher Hamann in the Überwasser churchyard

Hamann is the most truly Christian man I have ever met." But his sojourn in the bosom of the *familia sacra* was not destined to be a long one and it ended sadly. As the coach stood ready to take him to visit his friend Jacobi in Düsseldorf, he was called to his last journey. On June 21st 1788, a year to the day after he had left Königsberg, Hamann died surrounded by his friends of the *familia sacra*. Fürstenberg and Overberg wrapped his body in blankets and in the evening, by the light of torches, buried him in the princess's garden. This was the wish of Amalie von Gallitzin. For her, it was "an indescribably sweet thought to have in my garden the ashes of the blessed man, so great though so little known, so that near the grave in time to come, my children might breathe in something of the spirit of the dead man." She erected a dignified memorial to him, an urn on a square base, with the inscription: *viro christiano*, to the Christian. The monument was designed by Hemsterhuis, the Dutch philosopher. After the princess's death her house in Grüne Gasse was sold and the garden turned into a potato field; the grave of the great philosopher lay lonely and forgotten, until word of its neglected condition came to the ears of the king. Frederick William IV arranged for Hamann's grave to be transferred to the Überwasser cemetery.

THE FEAST OF ST. LAMBERT

If, instead of coming to Münster in December, Goethe had arrived in September, he, who could tell his hosts in Münster so much about Roman popular festivals, would also have had the opportunity to see an old Münster festival in celebration of the feast of St. Lambert, which dates back many years and is still celebrated today with as much vitality as ever. The visitor who arrives in Münster at the time of year when summer is drawing to a close, and when in the evenings autumn twilight falls early over the busily thronging streets, will meet with this strange scene: in old lanes and side streets and on open squares, he will

The celebration of the feast of St. Lambert
Oil painting by Bernhard Bröker (detail)

see pyramids of flowers decorated with candles. Round these,
children dance, singing special songs. "Lambertus sall liäwen, de
häff uss so leiff. Well dat nich kann miärken, dat is en dumm'n
Sleif." (Long live Lambert, who loves us so much. Who does
not realise that is a fool.) They sing old Münster folk songs with
question and answer. "Guter Freund, ich frage dir – Bester
Freund, was frägst du mir – Sag mir, was ist eine." (Good
friend, I ask you – Best friend, what do you ask me – Tell me
what is one.) Singing and dancing, address and rejoinder rise to
an excited climax with the arrival of a peasant with smock,
pipe and gnarled stick. He makes his way to the centre of the
circle and is greeted with the question "Farmer, farmer, how
much is your hay?" His hay costs a "Kiärmisskraun" – a Kirmes crown. And then in accordance with the instructions of
the song he chooses for himself out of the crowd singing and
dancing round him a Kirmes wife, a Kirmes servant-boy, a

Kirmes serving maid and a Kirmes child. Other old St. Lambert's day songs ring out. "Ein Edelmann ging zum Tore hinaus. Der Schäfer trieb seine Lämmerlein hinaus" (A noble-man went out through the city gate. The shepherd drove out his lambs) and "Der Herr, der schickt den Jäger aus, sollte die Birnen schmeissen" (The master who sends off the hunter should throw out the pears). And so it goes on until the candles of the pyramid die out and the groups of children disperse. Activities such as these on an evening in September follow an old Münster folk custom, probably the oldest one to have survived to the present day. Perhaps it is a reminder of the autumn day on which candles burn once again in the living rooms and work shops. Perhaps it goes back to an ancient Germanic festival of sun-worship which has been Christianised to become a feast in honour of St. Lambert, patron saint of the old town church. Near the church of St. Lambert a monument has been set up to celebrate this living custom.

THE GOLDEN COCKEREL

Once upon a time in ancient Rome, cackling geese aroused the Capitol and so saved the city from defeat. While the guards and even the dogs lay sleeping in the beleaguered citadel, the geese by their cackling awakened the captain of the guard, who in the very nick of time, was able to fend off an attack by the Gauls, who even at that moment were climbing up to the castle walls. It was not cackling geese but an excited cock which, as the story goes, saved the old town of Münster from imminent peril, and which is remembered to this very day. Once when the town was under siege and suffering great hardship and privation, an alderman decided that the time had come to kill his last cockerel. But at the last moment the wily cock, sensing what was in his master's mind, managed to escape. Understandably alarmed, crowing loudly and flapping his wings, he took refuge on the nearby Aegidius Gate. When the besieging forces encamped

93

outside the city walls saw this, their hearts sank and their hopes were dashed. They had thought that Münster was reduced to famine so terrible that before long the town would be forced to open her gates and surrender. But when they saw the cock sitting crowing on the Aegidius Gate, they assumed that there could be no question of shortage of food in the town, and so they marched away. The councillor who owned the bird was elected mayor by the grateful citizens. In recognition of the great service the cockerel had rendered to the town he had a silver statue of the bird made, which in the course of time became the object of high esteem and which is still to be seen today in the town treasury. In connection with the story, art historians have established the silver gilt cockerel as the work of the Nuremberg goldsmith Jörg Ruel (1598–1625). It can be opened and contains a large and a small drinking cup. It played an important part in a traditional drinking ceremony; every newly-elected burgomaster had to drink the health of the town by emptying the full cup (1 1/2 pints) in one draught. The golden cockerel is also used as the cup of honour of the town of Münster. Right up to the present day it is used to drink a toast to honoured guests.

MEMORIES OF PLAGUE AND FIRE

A more adequate form of protection than that of the legendary cockerel was provided by the watchman on the tower. Many times over the centuries the fire-bells have rung out their ominous message across the roofs of the town, warning the startled citizens of the danger which threatened their homes. In medieval towns there was cause to fear the spread of fires much more than in the towns of today with their brick buildings and fire-brigades. The flames would devour house after house with insatiable greed, sweeping from one narrow street to the next, and if the wind added its support, they were exceedingly difficult to quench. Münster was made to realise this time and

The silver-gilt cock in the Town Treasury in Münster

again. And if, in addition, the town was visited by famine or
the deadly, contagious plague, then the distress was twice as
great. And so it was in Münster in 1382. A devastating plague

The Plague Crucifix or the Black Christ in the cathedral (about 1480)

swept through the land. The old Bishop's Chronicle reported that „meer dan achte dusend lude" (more than 8,000 people) had fallen victim to it. This represents more than half the population of that time. But the disaster did not come alone. On a fateful Sunday in the following year the fire-bells in the church steeples began to peal. During a meeting of the Guild of Furriers and Tanners in an old inn near the church of St. Servatius, fire had broken out and, lashed by a strong wind, the flames spread with terrifying speed from roof to roof. Within a few hours 400 houses between the church of St. Servatius and the church of St. George were reduced to ashes, nor were the churches of St. Ludger or of St. Aegidius spared. The entire town would have gone up in flames but that, after anxious hours, heavy rains set in which checked the blaze. On the following day, a Monday, the bishop and the two burgomasters accompanied by the clergy and the members of the town council and all the citizens walked in a long procession of supplication and mourning round the scene of the great fire. This was Münster's first Great Procession, and ever since it has persisted as a pious custom, practised through six centuries, keeping alive the memory of that year of plague and fire.

THE SEND SWORD

"There is a deep significance in old customs." Three times during the year a great sword of execution is set up outside the town hall. It signifies the time of Send, Kirmes or the market-fair, which for more than 350 years has been marked by the sign of the sword. The Münster Send takes its name from the synod which the bishops used to summon twice a year. Just as crowds flocked to medieval religious festivals, so many people thronged to the Send tribunals which were held in the fore-court of the Cathedral (the Paradies), so providing the very conditions which favoured the development of large markets. Old chronicles report that in 1574 the council decided to place an executioner's sword on display on the town hall, as a token of jurisdiction over trading, just as in earlier days a market flag had been flown from the Cathedral. This Send sword is reminiscent of the sword held upright in his hand by Roland in the statue which stands in the market place in Bremen, and of similar ones

The *Send* sword as it is raised on the Town Hall on *Send* market days

in other north German towns. It had a two-fold significance: market privilege and jurisdiction. As long as it stood on the town hall, the market people could buy and sell freely and barter their wares unhindered. But it was also a symbol of stern jurisdiction and a warning to ruffians seeking to make trouble in the market. Anyone involved in brawling at a Send market, who caused bodily injury to another, had forfeited his life and had to atone by death. Later this severe ruling was relaxed. When the damage was not very great, the criminal could atone for it by paying a fine. Right up to this day, at times of Send, which date back to the spring synod in Lent, the feast of SS. Peter and Paul, patrons of the cathedral, in June, and the feast of the consecration of the church in October, the sword is placed on view outside the town hall, although no longer as a sign of jurisdiction. This practice which has persisted for centuries keeps alive a significant tradition: the upright sword is for us today the symbol of enduring order and justice.

THE WITHERED HAND

Delicate natures quail when, in the Hall of Peace in the town hall they catch sight of a strange, withered human hand. It lies on an old chest in which it has been kept for centuries. To judge from the painting and the iron mountings, the chest dates from the 16th century, that is, about the time of the Anabaptists. Probably the hand is just as old. Could it be a gruesome reminder of the Anabaptists? We do not know. Not a single line of written documentation nor any tradition passed down by word of mouth refers to it. An impenetrable veil of mystery surrounds this human hand, and to the question of who was its owner, and why it should have been placed in the town hall, no answer is given. For a long time it was believed to be the right hand of a notary who had had it cut off as punishment for having forged a document. Then the amputated hand was preserved as a terrible warning of stern retribution. Historical and legal experts hold a different view. They believe it to be a bodily token such as was customary in the administration of justice in medieval Germany before the introduction of Roman law. At that time, when someone was killed, it was customary practice in German law, when lodging an action for murder, not to bring the whole corpse before the court. Instead a finger or a hand was cut from the dead body in the presence of witnesses. This member then, together with the corroboration of the witnesses, served as a symbol of the slain man and as proof that the killing had indeed taken place. Could the withered hand be just such a token? Even that cannot be affirmed with certainty. But, we

The human hand preserved in the Town Hall for centuries

might argue, unless this hand had some particular significance and importance, it would not have been given a place in the town hall. And yet how strange it is that the story which it should serve to illustrate and preserve in the memory of posterity, is known to the hand alone.

THE HOUSE OF THE TWELVE MEN

An old town is rather like an old man. Both have a countenance marked by time from which one may glean much. The vicissitudes of life have left their indelible mark. In Münster there were certain well-weathered residential districts with quiet lanes which seemed to breathe with the life of the past. In ageing beauty they continued to serve just as they had done for many generations. Had they been able to speak what stories they could have told; but in stony silence they kept their secrets to themselves. What had they seen and known? Had love or hate, joy or sorrow dwelt beneath their crumbling roofs? Had happiness or misfortune visited there? Had life or death been the more frequent guest? Walking through the old lanes of the town, the visitor might ask himself all these questions, without finding any other answer but that both joy and sorrow, both birth and death had here, like anywhere else, each reigned in due season. But in Katthagen, in the Lane of the Twelve Men (Zwölfmännergasse) in the Überwasser district, there stood a house which had more to tell. It was called the House of the Twelve Men, because it provided shelter for twelve men in the evening of their lives. It was first mentioned in the 12th century as the foundation of a bishop. Originally it was exclusively a home for twelve servants of the chapter who, when their years of faithful service were at an end, moved in here as beneficiaries; but it was soon extended to include others. The twelve old men did not spend their last days neglected and forgotten, like inhabitants of a poor-house. They occupied a quite special position of honour as the result of a custom which persisted into this century. Once a year they walked in procession from the House of the Twelve Men to the Cathedral Square, and on Maundy Thursday they were the central figures of a Holy Week religious ceremony in the cathedral, in which the bishop himself washed and kissed their feet. Then the twelve old men returned to their home, to come back the following year, unless in the meantime death had carried off one of the little group. The depreciation of currency after the First World War put an end to the charitable foundation and the Second World War left behind it only the memory of the House of the Twelve Men.

GOOD MONDAY

Both in Münster and Vienna a tradition exists telling how, in the days of the Turkish Wars, Münster bakers saved Vienna from conquest by the Turks. While working one night in ground floor premises, the Münster bakers became aware that beneath them the Turks too were at work digging underground passages into the town. They reported their discovery to the Military Commandant of Vienna and so thwarted the plan of the Moslems. "It was bakers from Münster who in this way saved Vienna" were the words in an official invitation which the Münster Guild of Bakers received from Vienna 250 years later when the city was preparing a grand celebration of its liberation from the threat of the Turks. It is said that at the time the Emperor promised to the men who had saved his capital a reward of their own choosing. The Münster journeymen did not ask for gold but for a day's holiday on "Good Monday" which they used to celebrate in their home town of Münster as the feast day of their guild. Their request was granted, and when they returned to Münster from Vienna where as young journeymen travelling through the districts of Germany they must have been working out part of their time of service, the feast day of the Bakers Guild, Good Monday became in addition a celebration in memory of that historic event in Vienna when so much had been saved by the alertness of the journeymen. The Guild is firmly convinced of the truth of this tradition, although there is no historical proof. Once every three years Good Monday is celebrated as the proud feast of an ancient guild, with a Bakers' Queen and with flags flying, in the presence of the bishop, the governor of the province, the President and the chief burgomaster. It is not certain when the practice began, but it has certainly been in existence for more than 300 years. It probably had its roots in the spring holiday of the craftsmen's guilds and after the experience of the Münster bakers in Vienna took on the form in which it has come down to us today.

Flags flying on Good Monday / Oil painting by Theo Junglas

THE LAND OF HAM

In the poetic saga about the creation of the first Westphalians, the pig is the first creature to be mentioned: "And as the sole inhabitants of the country he found pigs, feeding upon the acorns in the woods" (Robert Hamerling). In his novel "The Adventures of Simplicius Simplicissimus" Grimmelshausen describes the delight of his hero at a Westphalian hearth where food hung to smoke. "O mirum! I saw the black sky filled with black lutes, flutes and fiddles, which turned out to be hams, sausages and sides of bacon hanging in the chimney; it cheered me up to look at them because it seemed to me that they were laughing with me." But it was Heinrich Heine who called Münsterland "the land of ham". But ham ist not the only pork product which is held in high esteem. During the summer months bacon served with fat beans is a popular dish in town and country. Who is there who respects the products of the land like the people of the Münster region? Their pumpernickel has been regarded by strangers with mixed feelings. Fabio Chigi, Papal legate to the Peace Congress was horrified at it ("Ecce panis westphalorum!") and the French novelist Flaubert called it "a gothick food", by which he did not refer to Gothic art but to the Goths of the migrations of the peoples. And indeed the bread eaten by the old Germanic tribes might well have been rather similar to this. Experts have ascribed the good health and the character of the Westphalians living in the district of Münster, along the Hellweg and round Osnabrück to the regular consumption of this hearty bread. This seems to have been the opinion too of the last Prince Bishop Max Franz, youngest son of the Empress Maria Theresia, of whom the French émigré Canon Baston wrote in his memoirs "that when he goes back home to Vienna he always packs as much pumpernickel as possible into his coach, so that he may continue as long as possible to have the pleasure of eating it."

THE HOSPITABLE HEARTH

The native of Münsterland is sometimes said to be taciturn, inhospitable and unsociable. Certainly he is not the most loquacious of men; his tongue must first be loosened and then he is able to spin a yarn as well as anyone. But none can deny his inborn sense of hospitality and good-natured sociability. If this had not been so, he would not have made the hearth the focal point of his home where the members of the household, guests and neighbours could gather together to enjoy warmth and conversation. Social gatherings took place round the open fire. It was too the main feature of the Münster Altbierküche, which developed, with very few changes, from the traditional Westphalian peasant kitchen. The Altbierküche is a symbol of old Münster and of its relaxed sociability. Here craftsmen and

In Pinkus Müller's Altbier-Kitchen / Oil painting by Eugen Fernholz

lawyers, young students and old ones sat together in one cheer-
ful circle in which they were all equally welcome guests, and
more than one of them has carved in the smooth table-top how
his enjoyment here has matched that in Auerbachs Keller. The
Altbierküche was named after Münster's famous Altbier, made
from hops, malt and surface-fermented yeast according to an
ancient brewing process, and which achieves its somewhat sour
taste by long storage. At one time every Altbierküche had its
own Altbier brewery. At about the middle of the last century
400 Altbier inns still existed, half a century later only 41
remained and of these only one survived the First World War.
This was largely the result of the new supply of mains water
which was introduced in 1880. Well-water which had previously
been in general use in Münster had not been entirely safe, but
now, in addition to Altbier, the citizens had a supply of good,
safe drinking-water. Then came the First World War with its

shortages and privations, when the breweries received only a limited allocation of grain. And in addition, the great copper vats from the breweries had to be given up for the sake of their precious metal. Small breweries were hit particularly hard. So it is not difficult to understand why, in face of such adverse conditions, only one survived to carry on the tradition of brewing and serving Altbier. It was owned by Jans Müller and his son Carl, popularly known as Pinkus. Old Münster lives on in his Altbierküche. A huge hearth dominates the tap-room, and above it are suspended great, savoury-smelling hams. Old Westphalian household furniture decorates the rooms of the tavern. Rush-seated chairs stand round oak tables, pewter plates and pitchers gleam on dressers and shelves and great tankards for Altbier hang above the bar. And on the wooden beams of the ceiling such memorable rhymes as these are inscribed:

> Dat man dat Drinken nich to bieten bruk,
> Dat is doch mähr äs prächtig.
> Ick faoll de Hände üövern Buk
> Un priese Gott andächtig.
> (That one can take drink without biting it
> Is more than splendid.
> I fold my hands across my belly
> And praise God piously.)

CRAZY BARON GISBERT VON ROMBERG

If we were looking for a character from recent times to rival that waggish trickster of the 14th century Till Eulenspiegel, Münster could offer two promising candidates: Crazy Baron von Romberg and his contemporary, Professor Landois, whose fame extended far beyond Münster and Westphalia. The wow of a Baron, who lived in the second half of the 19th century in his moated castle in Münsterland, from which he used to ride into Münster on horseback, was a real-life Eulenspiegel to equal any to be found in legend. The stories which are told of his high-spirited

The crazy baron leaps the table
Oil painting by Fritz Grotemeyer in the Restaurant Ägidiihof

pranks and escapades often seem quite incredible, but eye-witnesses and their descendants assure us that they are true, even if in the course of time, poets and yarn-spinners who delight in tall stories may have added much to reinforce the original facts. A wealth of traditional tales has grown up round this figure who appealed so greatly to the imagination of the people. The setting for most of the mad baron's escapades was the "Etablissement of the Master-baker Louis Midy". Gisbert von Romberg's companions at his drinking parties were his fellow officers of the Münster cuirassiers. Old accounts still preserved, prove that he was a prodigal drinker and a lavish spender. A series of pictures painted by Fritz Grotemeyer, which today hang in the restaurant Ägidiihof, illustrate some of his heroic deeds. Once Romberg, dressed in princely attire, made his way into town to the accompaniment of a flourish of trumpets, in a coach drawn by six horses, and halting in the Roggenmarkt, he allowed himself to be shaved sitting high up on the box of his coach, in order to provide a vivid illustration of a remark made by a member of the Chamber of Deputies: "The Westphalian aristocracy does not climb down to the people." On another occasion he rode his horse up the steps into his favourite restaurant and across the well-filled tables, to the horror of the assembled guests, among whom only Landois was equal to the situation. With a ready wit he greeted the baron with "Kiek, dao kümp dat Rossbäff!" (Look! here comes the joint!)

THE MERRY PROFESSOR

At the edge of the Zoological Gardens stands a curious building not unlike a castle keep. This is the Tuckesburg where Professor Landois 'lived in his individualistic fashion as Wildgraf Tucks. His pupil Hermann Löns called him a true man of the people and a symbol of Westphalia. This Westphalian Till Eulenspiegel was basically a scientist. It is difficult to believe that a man who could indulge in so much buffoonery could yet produce such important and significant work. Like Faust, Landois could say that he had studied "even alas theology too"; from theology he turned to zoology and became a scientist of considerable fame, honoured by scientific circles at home and abroad with one distinction after another; he founded the Zoological Garden

Professor Hermann Landois inaugurates his own memorial

and the Museum of Natural Science and in addition wrote many scientific works as well as stories and plays in Low German; he assembled a group of kindred spirits to indulge in secret feasts of bears' paws, and the stories of the varied Sunday afternoon entertainments which he used to provide for young and old alike, in order to make a success of his Zoological Garden are still retold with great enjoyment today by grey-haired citizens of Münster. He did everything for his Zoological Garden, the origins of which are surely as bizarre as any in the world. First he organised evenings of card-games. The profits went into a "monkey fund". More evenings of card-games followed, until the profits were sufficient to build cages to house the guinea-pigs. Then in order to raise money more quickly, he arranged theatrical productions in Low German dialect. In his later years Professor Landois crowned all his earlier jokes by having a commemorative monument to himself erected outside his Tuckesburg, while he was still alive, and dressed in the very same clothes and standing in just the same attitude as the statue of the memorial, he himself made the inaugural speech. To all humourless critics he provided a typical Landois reply in advance in a lengthy poem in Low German dialect which is inscribed on the monument:

> Well't seihn will, kumm un kiek't sik an,
> Et iss nich to verachten,
> Un well't von vüörn nich lieden kann,
> Mag't Achterdehl betrachten!
> (Anyone who wants to see, come and take a look,
> It is not to be scorned,
> And anyone who does not like the front view
> Is welcome to look at the back!)

THE GIANT AMMONITES

In the glass-roofed court of the Museum of Natural Science which Hermann Landois founded, and which contains valuable collections from the present-day and pre-historic animal and

The Seppenrade giant ammonite in the Museum of Natural Science

plant world, the two famous giant Seppenrade ammonites are on display. The larger one is some $8\frac{1}{2}$ ft. high and weighs 70 cwt. It is believed to be the largest ammonite ever to have been found. In 1895 it was excavated in a quarry near Seppenrade to the south of Münster and brought to Münster. Although ammonites in their petrified state have the appearance of snails, they in fact belong to the genus cephalopods. They had lived at the place where they were found some 60 million years ago. Thus the Seppenrade ammonites are a reminder of primitive times when Münsterland was still covered by seas inhabited by cuttle-fish and giant molluscs such as these.

111

THE "KIEPENKERL"

The "Kiepenkerl" stands today as a token of the good, simple Biedermeier age with its quiet and comfort which the Mad Baron and the Merry Professor took pleasure in disturbing. He started his career as the rural messenger for the district round Münster, acting as the agent in trade between town and country. But he could not keep up with modern developments in traffic and trade. He, in his hob-nailed boots, was no match for railways and motor-lorries. But in early days, men like him had wandered all the world over, seeking their fortune far from their native hearth. These travelling merchants from the north of Münsterland were known as "Tödden". The name means something like "birds of passage". Soon they laid aside the "Kiepe", the basket which they carried on their back, and took to travelling the land in canvas-covered tilt-carts. But they never forgot to return home from time to time even if their trade had prospered abroad and made them rich. The heritage of their native land was implanted too deeply in their hearts for that. Even when they became great merchants, no longer merely carrying local products in a basket, they remained fundamentally "Kiepenkerle", itinerant traders. Many a proprietor of a large trading company which is today wealthy and influential at home and abroad, can trace his family tree back to a "Tödden" or "Kiepenkerl", and is proud to have such an ancestor. It is fitting that Münster should have erected a statue to the "Kiepenkerl". It stands in the Spiekerhof in front of a group of small, newly-built gable-houses which are in harmony with it as it is with them. He is holding a pipe and a knotted stick and wearing a cap, neckerchief and a long smock, while on the ground beside him lies the small basket with a handle which he used to carry on his arm. Most important of all, on his back is his Kiepe or portable hamper filled with local products such as eggs, butter, vegetables, hares, ham and other good things which he is taking to market in Münster. His statue was damaged

The *Kiepenkerl* in front of the new gabled houses

during the war, but it was not long before his fellow-countrymen set it up again. At its unveiling in Autumn 1953, the President of the Republic, Theodor Heuss took the opportunity to pay the town of Münster a great compliment when he said: "Whenever I visit a beautiful German town I always say it is the second most beautiful town in Germany, whether it is Bamberg or Bremen. This always provokes the question, which is the most beautiful. And then I say: Münster."

THE MERCERS GUILD HALL

Early in the Middle Ages, merchants from Münster began to travel abroad to Flanders and England, and to the Scandinavian countries as far as Gotland and Livonia. They contributed much to the great work of colonising the German lands in the east and building up Hanseatic trade with distant countries, achievements which resulted from the energy and vision of the North Germans. However far afield the Hanse merchants might be active, in Bruges and Bergen, in Lübeck and London, in Danzig and Wisby, in Reval and Novgorod, traders from Münster were amongst them. They were indeed so numerous and strong that in Riga, as the merchants of Lübeck and Soest had done, they were able to found a trade settlement of their own known as the Münster Court or the "Great Chamber of Münster", where the Westphalian merchants could find accomodation for themselves and their goods. Out of the profits made as members of the Hanseatic league from successful foreign trade, many of the merchants of Münster built themselves splendid houses in the Prinzipalmarkt and contributed much to the prosperity of the medieval town. Even at that time, 450 years ago, they planned to link Münster to the sea by a canal. Their fine Guild Hall, the Krameramtshaus, dating from the year 1588, still stands today on the Alter Steinweg. The traditional motto of the Münster merchants "Ehr iss dwang gnog" (Honour is spur enough) is inscribed above the fireplace in the main hall. When

the Peace Congress brought high politics to Münster, the houses
of the curia, the mansions of the nobility, the guild houses and
the houses of the leading merchants had to be placed at the

disposal of the ambassadors. Between 1646 and 1648, the Mercers Guild Hall provided accommodation for the ambassadors of the Netherlands.

IN ITS 387th YEAR

Only two houses away from the Mercers Guild Hall, in the shadow of St. Lambert's Church stands an even older example of domestic architecture, the house on the corner of Alter Steinweg and Alter Fischmarkt. The form in which it has been preserved dates back to the end of the Anabaptist period. Its ornamental frontage with late Gothic tracery and a fine oriel window is greatly admired. The building houses Münster's oldest book shop and press, which has a quite remarkable history. At about the time the house was built, plans were being made in Münster for a venture into the new "black art". In 1591 Lambert Raesfeldt, under patents granted by the Elector, founded a printing office in the buildings of the former Tzwyvel Press (see p. 63) which soon began to make a name for itself. From the beginning his aim had been to print the Holy Scriptures "in düsser Sassenschen oder Westfälischer sprake" (in this Saxon or Westphalian tongue). By the time he died in 1617 he had (as Bernhard Lucas points out in his thesis), published no fewer than 207 works in Latin, German and Low German. His work was consistently encouraged by the Prince Bishop and the Cathedral Chapter. When the number of pupils at the Cathedral School had grown to over 1100, and it was moved to new, more extensive premises in Johannisstrasse, to become the Paulinum Grammar School, Lambert Raesfeldt was allowed to set up his officium typographicum in the rooms formerly occupied by the Cathedral School on the Horsteberg. On 10th January 1595 the Cathedral Chapter concluded an agreement of tenure with him. This lease and its duration are without parallel in the history of German publishing. From 1595 to 1945, through good times and bad, both parties observed the

In the shadow of St. Lambert's Church: an old book shop

terms of the contract with unequalled fidelity. For 350 years
Lambert Raesfeldt and his successors carried on their business
on the Horsteberg below the cathedral until the building was
destroyed by bombs during the war. Throughout the whole of
its long existence, the business always passed from father to son
or daughter, and has remained in the same family for 387 years.
Since 1823 the firm founded by Lambert Raesfeldt has been

known as the Regensberg Press. But the true age of the firm is measured by its *Münsterischer Almanach*, remarkable as a piece of social history and unique amongst almanacs. It is already in its 387th year and is believed to be the oldest almanac in Germany.

BEYOND THE GATES OF THE TOWN

"Just as Königsberg was once called the town of pure reason, one could, indeed one must call Münster the town of pure geniality. How agreeable life used to be there. Nowhere was family life more good-natured; nowhere was it more pleasant to stroll than in the arcades of Münster which afforded a charming setting for tender interludes between young lovers; nowhere else could one sit in a tavern at such ease with never a thought for work or business; nowhere else could one so often enjoy a gentle stroll to the nearest coffee-house beyond the town walls, to indulge in such fine coffee, such splendid current-bread, such delicious milk and such satisfying ham-sandwiches." This is how Münster and the citizens of Münster at the turn of the century appeared to Hermann Löns who spent much of his youth and student days in the house of the Knights of St. John near the Buddenturm. It is rather like a belated Biedermeier genre-painting drawn with a touch of irony but with a great deal of personal affection for this way of life. The people of Münster clung to the old custom which had become dear to them of making leisurely excursions on foot along lonely tracks and romantic paths through field and meadow to one of the many hospitable coffee-gardens round Münster, where according to the custom of the country, they would take some refreshment, and well-satisfied with themselves and their native Münsterland, would make their way home again. Whereas at the turn of the century these walks rarely took them very far beyond the town walls, as time went on they extended deeper into the country as far as the Werse, Angel and Ems.

The Rüschhaus near Münster / Droste-Hülshoff-Museum

ANNETTE'S HERMITAGE

In the course of such rambles, nothing is more delightful than to come upon the solitary home of the country's greatest woman poet. In 1743 the master-builder Johann Conrad Schlaun (1694–1773), Director of Building and Principal Engineer to the Prince Bishop, and in addition Major General and Supreme

Commander of the Münster Artillery, acquired from Count Plettenberg an estate in the country, on which between 1745 and 1748 he built an idyllic country-house and two neighbouring buildings. The house clearly has its architectural origins in the traditional Münsterland farmhouse and it has refined this style to artistic perfection. The Rüschhaus lies withdrawn in peaceful seclusion in the Münsterland countryside, surrounded by high woods and quiet meadows. Water-lilies bloom on the miniature moat. Putti daydream in the park. After the master-builder, the great poetess made her home here. Annette von Droste's birthplace was the nearby moated castle of Hülshoff where she was born on 10th January 1797, and she died on 24th May 1848 in Meersburg Castle on Lake Constance, but her real home was the Rüschhaus. In 1826, after the death of her father, Annette together with her mother and sister moved into this house which her father had bought for the family to use after he died. She lived there for twenty years and there she wrote most of her poetry. Once a week a servant woman was sent to Münster on errands such as delivering letters and fetching books, and occasionally she was visited by close friends, but otherwise, apart from her visits to the Rhine or the Lake of Constance, Annette lived undisturbed in her solitary home which was "full of peace and sunshine, the trill of the lark and the song of the nightingale." Levin Schücking, for years her closest friend, described Germany's greatest woman poet and her secluded life in the Rüschhaus: "There was something strange, elfin about this ethereal creature who had such spiritual refinement and was delicate to the point of being incorporeal. She was almost like a being from a fairy-tale. Her remarkably finely moulded, high, broad forehead was surrounded by a wealth of light golden hair which she wore drawn up in a high crown on top of her head. Her nose was long and finely modelled. Particularly beautiful was her small delicate mouth, and when she spoke her lips moved with such grace revealing small, pearl-like teeth. She had a tendency to hold her head slightly inclined forward as if her

Annette von Droste Hülshoff / Picture by J. Sprick

slight body were scarcely able to hold it upright, or perhaps it was the result of her habit of bringing her rather short-sighted eyes quite close to objects she was observing. But from time to time she would raise her head and fix her steady gaze directly on the person she was addressing; and particularly when she made a humorous observation or jest, she would raise her head in laughter, and when she was gay her face would take on a degree of joyous self-assurance, an innocent high-spiritedness which would shine out of her exceptionally large, clear blue eyes which for all their good humour were very penetrating."

121

Post wind-mill and mill-house on the edge of Lake Aa
on the Sentruper Höhe

Levin Schücking also captured for us the magic of the peaceful countryside where he would frequently visit his dear friend in the "little estate". "It was enveloped in a peace and tranquillity all its own. Everywhere the view was bounded by nearby woods, high hedges and rows of trees. Only at rare intervals is it possible to glimpse a more distant prospect of an enclosed field, the corner of a meadow and a row of blue hills beyond. No sound interrupts this stillness, save perhaps the neighing of a horse as a team of four draws the plough through the heavy clods of loamy soil in a neighbouring field, or the quacking of ducks as they feed on the duckweed in the narrow moat, or the cackling of a hen as, with head inclined, it catches sight of the hawk circling noiselessly, high above the oak-trees. It would be easy to forget, in this rustic retreat, that outside, beyond the encircling woods, there exists another world, a world of agitation and clamour."

As one returns from the Rüshhaus idyll the town picture on the horizon is much the same as that which greeted Annette as she rode into Münster. The distant scene of spires and towers has hardly changed, except for the towering highrise Halls of Residence for students, that have sprung up alongside the church towers. Not that the previous generations were idle and left no marks behind them. They have extended the town, as they thought right and fitting, in the style and spirit of the age, which invariably, when a generation is inspired, is a heavenly gift;

The new Municiple Theatre, Münster. Sideview.

The new town hall

but if it is not, can be a disaster. Münster has grown and changed since Annette's day. Neo-Gothic churches and schools, railway stations and post offices have been built. But theyhave railway stations and post offices have been built. But the have had little effect on the architectural form of the town. In the meantime much has been destroyed, making way for new buildings. The decade following the most destructive war in history, presented great opportunities. Building had to be carried out on such a scale as never before. Here it would have been easy for the spirit of the age to come into conflict with the spirit of past ages. Münster is a town with tradition which is also alive to new developments and able to cherish and transform traditional values. With its great history and culture it stands in the centre of the stream of time. Here too, life puts on one growth ring after the other. In addition to restoring faithfully many revered architectural and artistic monuments, Münster has been able to produce some fine examples of elegant modern architecture. They are spoken of in terms of highest praise, particularly, the new Municiple Theatre, the Chamber of Agriculture, the All Weather Zoo, the University Clinics and Science Institutes, and not least, the new Provincial Bank.

THE LAKE AA

Münster is situated on the River Aa. This river collects the water from the Baumbergen and sends it, flowing through the Werse and the Ems, into the North Sea. In dry seasons the River Aa is just a tiny brook, no obstacle to the hiker. He can jump over it comfortably. But in wet seasons or with melting snow it has always been dangerous. It then carries more water than the river bed can cope with. The result is, or was, that the cellars of the town have been under water, and the meadows in front of Aegiditor flooded. Then it needed only black frost to turn the area into a glassy ice rink, and beckon skating fans to "Münster's favourite pleasure". Much has been written about

this, for instance by O. H. Brückmann, who in Paderborn in 1863 published a book: "Old and New from Münsterland and its Environs". He wrote: "Between Aegiditor and Abschnittstor stretches a meadow half a mile long and twenty minutes broad, which from autumn to spring is flooded when the tiny river Aa overflows its banks. Scarcely has a thin layer of ice formed on this expanse of water when it becomes on weekday and Sunday afternoons for a good part of Münster's population, old and young, gentle and simple, men and boys, women and girls, a rendez-vous to indulge their favourite pleasure – skating and sledding".

Skating before the Gates of Münster has even found its way into Opera literature. The French playwright, Eugen Scribe (author of the famous comedy "A Glass of Water"), has written a libretto, "The Prophet" (Jan van Leiden). This libretto is the theme of Giacomo Meyerbeer's opera of the same name, which had its première in the big Opera House in Paris in 1849, and in the following year, in the great German Opera Houses of Hamburg, Dresden, Munich and Breslau. Scribe had never seen the Münster girls on skates, but he had heard about them, and dedicated a few rhythmic verses to those of them who used to take food to soldiers, on skates. Meyerbeer elevated this choir-song to a lovely skating ballet. This aesthetical and sportive preamble is a prelude to what can come out of the flooded and frozen meadows of the Aa. Professor Hermann Landois also belonged to a group of skating enthusiasts. It was his idea to collect the seasonally inconstant waters of the Aa into a reservoir. Time and time again the Münster authorities considered his suggestion, but always lacked the courage to execute it. For, who would pay for it all? If Münster did not have the Lord Mayor Sperlich it would not have the Lake Aa today. In the 1920's they began to scoop out the Aa meadows and transform the tiny brook into a sizeable lake. Not only the local people and the pedestrians rejoice over this event, today. The lake has attracted water-sportsmen and women. It has become a favourite sport and playground for paddlers, sailors, and rowers. A special wharf on Lake Dümmer got the contract to build a swish waterbus to take over the traffic between the Golden Bridge an the All Weather Zoo. The only stop on this run is Theo Breider's Windmill Farm.

THE WINDMILL FARM

It would be worth your while to stop off at this Windmill Farm. There is no better example of what a Citizens' Action Group can achieve when prompted by sheer love of a cause and led by the right man. Theo Breider (like Hermann Landois) is a unique presence in Münster and Westphalian life. He is a dynamic personality of singularly inexhaustible energy, as if driven

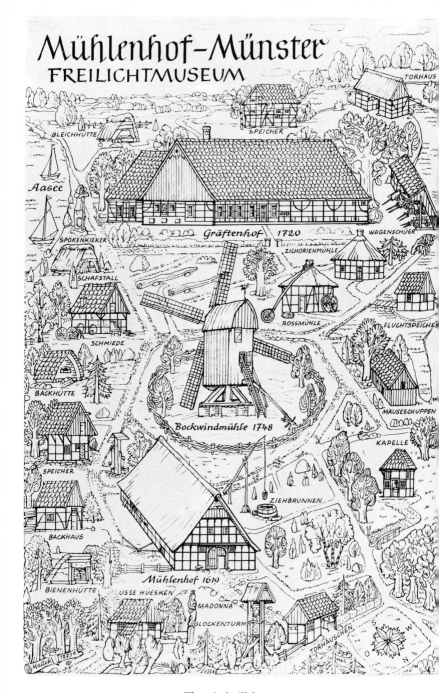

The windmill farm

by a multi-horse-powered engine. Above all, he has the great gift as a speaker that enables him to convince people of all classes, to inspire them, and cajole them into cooperating, regardless of self-interest, in the realization of his plans. That is the secret of the success of his work. Practically all of the buildings that comprise Windmill Farm have been donations, including the Trestle-Windmill itself. Likewise, the stock and the collections of folklore museum pieces have been given gratis. The donors are many. Finding volunteers for each special task of the construction operation was no problem for Theo Breider. Building contractors and tradesmen, students and soldiers, police and firemen, also British and Dutch military units were at his disposal to help him with the project. So there since 1960 is the Windmill Farm in a multi-building layout, an Open Air Museum with a rich collection of object relics of local peasant life. But best of all is the living spirit emanating from this rustic cell to the urban metropolis of Westphalia. The Windmill Farm has become a meeting place of international dimension.

THE ALL WEATHER ZOO

The Westphalian Zoological Garden on the Himmelreichallee in Münster is no more. When it was 99 years old the animals were moved out, and the cages and fences were demolished. It was an operation that saddened many Münster citizens. The West German Provincial Bank needed the site, and who could have resisted them? One had to bow to the inevitable and be consoled by the argument that the old Zoo was, in any case, too small, and no possibility could be seen for further development. Now all that has changed. The animals have got new homes, and there is no lack of space where they live on Sentruper Höhe. The new Zoo is laid out on a site of 30 hectare (74 acres) and has room for 2000 animals. It is supposed to be the most modern Zoo in the world as well as the one and only all weather Zoo. The name quickly became popular. It does not

refer to the inmates of the Zoo, but to the visitors. They can visit this Zoo in all weathers without fear of getting caught in the rain. They walk along dry, roofed-over paths. The All Weather Zoo exercises an extraordinary attraction which extends far beyond Westphalia. In a few months no less than a million visitors were recorded. They had come from all parts of Germany from Hamburg to Frankfurt. They were full of praise for it. But anyone who thinks that too many tons of concrete were wasted on it should count the many preserved and newly planted trees on the site. Since they are favoured biologically and grow, they will soon put the concrete constructions in the shade in both senses of the term.

THE BANK ON THE AA

What has become of the former Zoo site? Here stands a very new building that does not look to be the continuation of a traditional institution which occupies just as cherished a place in the history and structure of Münster as does the founding of the Zoo by Professor Landois. The interesting historical background ought not to be forgotten. When, after the Battle of Leipzig concern was focused on defeating decisively the disturbing factor of Europe in France itself, not only Prussian and Russian but also Danish and Swedish regiments marched through Westphalia. Some of them were in no hurry, doing only "short day marches and several rest days", so that the civilian Governor von Vincke suspected the Swedes of "intentional hesitancy", that "these troops do not make contact with the enemy too soon". Actually, they were not there in time to help Blücher and Wellington defeat the French at Waterloo. On their way back they again marched through Westphalia, and once again the towns, villages and hamlets had to feed the hungry soldiers and horses. But the Swedes did not forget that, and twelve years later they paid the bill. They transferred 258 703 thaler, 12 silver shillings and 7 pence to the King of

Provincial Bank and Building Society Savings Bank

Prussia for the food and coach horses requisitioned by their troops. His Majesty's Government informed the President v. Vincke that the money was at his disposal. The President was of the opinion, however, that a just distribution among the real claimants was just not possible now. He suggested that the money be used to found a Credit Bank which would help the communities with loans to build roads and schools, and for the reclamation of land. Berlin agreed, and so in 1832 the Westphalian Provincial Credit Bank was founded. Without the Swedish payment it would never have existed. From this Credit Bank, which soon as Central Receiving Bank took over the payment of interest on saving accounts of all Westphalian

Saving Banks, sprung the big Provincial Bank of Westphalia. When a spacious new building was needed the architect in charge, Harald Deilmann, who also designed the All Weather Zoo, had a brain wave. One can only wonder at and admire the unusual but original type of architecture, magnificently set in the landscape, rising in terraces, marvellously structured inside and outside. Here a building has been erected which is inimitable in the artistic individuality it presents. This Bank on the Aa is a treasure of modern architecture, a unique sight of modern times.

THE WATCHMAN ON THE TOWER OF ST. LAMBERT'S

Münster is full of curiosities! This statement has remained true although much has changed in the course of time. It was possible to restore much that appeared lost, because it had lived on in the memory of the people. An example of this is the watchman on the tower of St. Lambert's. How often had we heard him as we returned home through the streets of Münster in the evening or during the night. When the sound of his horn rang out to the four winds over old Münster, it was as if we could feel the very breath of the venerable *Westphalic metropolis*. Then the sirens of war drowned the notes of his horn and bombs destroyed his room in the tower. The watchman himself died during the war and no-one knew what became of his horn. If the tower watchman had been no more than a romantic trapping he would certainly have passed into oblivion. But he was so much a part of the history and the character of the town, so much a part of its living tradition, that in 1950 he was able once again to take up his post as the "highest" official of the town. The office has up his post as the "highest" official of the town. The office has existed for five hundred years. The watchman is first mentioned in documents dating from 1481. Over the centuries many watchmen have been appointed, but many too have been relieved of their office and thrown into prison for having neglected their

The watchmans view of the Prinzipalmarkt

duties and endangered the town. In his oath of office the watchman had to swear to maintain a watchful vigil over the town and surrounding countryside, and not only to sound his horn at the stroke of each new hour, but also to watch for outbreaks of fire and to give the guards at the gates timely warning of the

The tower-watchman of St. Lambert's sounds out each passing hour over the sleeping town

approach of enemy troops on foot or on horseback. In 1777 the town council declared that "the safety of the town depends entirely on the watchman on the tower". The town gave him many other duties. Most people have almost forgotten that he also had charge of a glockenspiel in the tower which used to play before the hour struck. Now once again the tower watch man sounds his horn. As the symbolic representative of the town authorities in charge of the well-being of the citizens, he has once again taken his place high up near the cages of the Anabaptists, and every night on the stroke of each hour, the sound of his horn rings out over the town which has risen from ruins to advance into the future without ever forgetting the way it has come.

Peace thaler of 1648

FROM THE ANNALS OF THE TOWN

792 · Charlemagne sent the Friesian missionary Liudger to win western Saxony or Westphalia for Christianity. Liudger who was the first bishop of Münster from 805 to 809, built a *monasterium* at Mimigernaford, a farming community in the old land of the Bructeri, on a hill by the river Aa, and surrounded it with a protective wall and ditch. This *monasterium* was not a monastic establishment in the narrow sense but a canonical house in which Liudger with clergy and pupils lived a communal life according to the teachings of Chrodegang. The *regula canonicorum* of the church reformer Archbishop Chrodegang of Metz followed basically the rule of the order of St. Benedict. This explains the use of the term *monasterium* although it did not refer to the house of a monastic order.

1040 · The great Imperial visit. Henry III with leading figures of state (the Archbishops of Mainz, Cologne, Magdeburg and Bremen, the Bishops of Bamberg, Minden, Hildesheim, Osnabrück, Lüttich, Zeitz and Schleswig) visited Bishop Hermann I, celebrated Christmas with him in Münster and took part in the establishment of the Church and Foundation of Our Lady (Überwasser). During the Imperial visit the Bishop of Bamberg, later to become Pope Clement II was consecrated in Münster Cathedral by the Archbishop of Mainz.

1090 · Bishop Erpho completed and consecrated the second cathedral building of which parts of the western fabric are still preserved.

1110 · Bishop Burchard, Imperial Chancellor, who befriended the Emperors Henry IV and Henry V in the Investiture Contest, extended the Cathedral Close southwards as far as the Rothenburg and surrounded it with a strong protective wall.

1121 · Duke Lothar of Supplinburg who later became Emperor, conquered Münster causing great devastation.

1150 · A most important decision for Münster's urban development: the Bishop abandoned the fortification of the Bishop's Castle and instead threw a rampart and moat round the whole town. The rampart which until then had surrounded the Bishop's Castle was divided into small plots and made available for building, while at the same time foundations were laid for the fortifications of the medieval town which can still be seen today in the rampart promenade.

1156 · The great Hohenstaufen Emperor Barbarossa visited the See of Münster to celebrate the festival of Easter with his friend Bishop Frederick II. The two men remained close friends during the whole of their lives. Both were enthroned on the same day and at the same place, one as king, the other as bishop. This took place in 1152 in the Imperial town of Aachen. After his visit Barbarossa appointed the provost of Münster Cathedral as his Chancellor. This provost became the greatest chancellor of the medieval empire. His name was Rainald von Dassel.

1180 · With the fall of Henry the Lion, Duke of Saxony and the partition of his ducal lands, his authority was at an end. The Bishop of Münster himself became ruler and Prince Bishop.

1253 · In accordance with the economic policy of the Hanseatic League, Münster entered an alliance with the towns of Dortmund, Lippstadt and Soest for the protection of commercial traffic and the extension of foreign trade, in which Münster played a leading rôle until the time of the Thirty Years War.

1264 · The third cathedral building, most of which still stands today, was started in 1225 and completed under Bishop Gerhard von der Mark who consecrated the new building.

1350 · The Gothic Town Hall on the Prinzipalmarkt was completed at about the middle of the century.

1382/3 · The years of plague and fire. The first Great Procession.

1500 · Rudolf von Langen, provost of the cathedral, made Münster a renowned stronghold of humanism.

1534/5 · The rule of the Anabaptists and their downfall.

1643 · In the Thirty Years War, Münster was recognised internationally as a neutral town. Emperor Ferdinand declared it free of all "allegiance to His Imperial Majesty and to the State". The Bishop, as ruling prince, did the same. The great Peace Congress began.

1661 · As the setting of the Peace Congress, the town had been free of all obligations towards Emperor and ruling prince; it now sought once again to become directly subject only to the Emperor, and it was humiliated by the ruling prince Christoph Bernhard von Galen. He had a notice put up on the communal guild house, the *Schoehus,* bearing the message "Cobbler! stick to your last!" and he reduced the Town Hall to a military guard house. The days of middle-class power were over. The period of absolute rule by the nobility began. New building was mainly commissioned by the aristocracy (Baroque churches and mansions for the nobility).

1757 · During the Seven Years War, as the result of an alliance entered into by its ruler, the Elector Clemens August of Cologne, Münster stood on the side of the French and of the Emperor, against the Prussians, the Hannoverians and the English. In 1757 the town was occupied by the French.

1758 · Prussian and English forces occupied Münster.

1759 · The French re-conquered the city. A siege followed and the town was heavily bombarded by Prussian and Hannoverian artillery. The district round the Church of St. Martin suffered particularly severe damage. 200 houses, the Lotharingian Monastery and the tower of the Church of St. Martin went up in flames. The stricken town changed hands again. The French retreated and the Prussians took over.

1764 · Franz von Fürstenberg, the Electoral Minister for the See of Münster ordered the dismantling of the fortifications. The entire ring of fortifications which enclosed the town, with its eleven gates, was pulled down; the inner rampart was given over to building, the outer rampart was converted into a promenade. Only the Buddenturm and the Zwinger were preserved.

1767 · The building of the palace was begun. It continued until 1773.

1775 · The Playhouse was opened by the Elector.

1780 · In April 1780 teaching began in the University of Münster. There were four faculties with a total of eleven professors; the Faculty of Medicine had only one professor.

1792 · Goethe visited the "Münster circle".

1794 · The town gave shelter to 1100 French émigrés.

1802 · Blücher marched into Münster with three battalions and a regiment of Hussars, to seize it for Prussia. The Cathedral Chapter protested in vain. The Imperial Commission had decided to dissolve the ecclesiastical states of Münster and Paderborn and incorporate them into Westphalia.

1806 · The Prussians withdrew. Napoleon's troops occupied the town.

1810 · Münster was apportioned to the French Empire.

1811 · By a decree of Napoleon's all monasteries and religious foundations were abolished. In 23 churches no more services were held. The Cathedral Square became a drill ground. Conscription was strictly enforced. The guillotine stood in the courtyard of the cathedral.

1813 · On 6th November, following Napoleon's defeat at Leipzig, the first Cossacks arrived in Münster. They were allies in the fight against Napoleon and were seeking provisions. They refused meat, demanding instead live cattle which they slaughtered themselves. They were followed by more Russian and Prussian regiments.

1815 · Münster became capital of the Province of Westphalia.

1818 · The faculties of Medicine and Law in the University were closed in favour of the newly founded University of Bonn. (This was the origin of the proverb: Bonn's reins are made of Münster leather.) In Münster there remained only a college which later became an Academy of Theology and Philosophy.

1826 · The first representative Assembly of the Province of Westphalia was opened in the palace in Münster by the Marshal of the Diet, Baron vom Stein. This was the beginning of the movement towards self-government which finally led to the formation of the Westphalian Provincial Union (Provinzialverband) and later of the Regional Union (Landschaftsverband) of Westphalia-Lippe.

1848 · The stretch of railway Münster-Hamm was opened.

1853 · For the first time the streets of Münster were lit by gas-light.

1855 · In this year Münster's population numbered 22,450. The municipal authorities included: 1 chief burgomaster, 1 deputy mayor and 6 town councillors, 1 town clerk with 1 registrar and 1 clerk, 1 municipal treasurer, 1 police inspector, 1 commissioner of police, 1 secretary of police; as lesser officials: 1 inspector of buildings, 1 town hall janitor, 2 town servitors, 4 police sergeants, 1 gaoler, 1 theatre manager, 1 tower watchman, 5 night-watchmen, 7 watchmen at the gates, 4 supervisors of wood and coal measures, 1 supervisor of charcoal and chalk measures, 1 town crier.

1875 · Professor Landois, with the help of his evening socials, founded the Zoological Garden.

1880 · Inauguration of Münster's municipal water supply.

1899 · With the construction of the Dortmund-Ems Canal, Münster was connected by water to the Ruhr and the North Sea.

1902 · A Faculty of Law and Political Science was added to the Royal Academy of Theology and Philosophy and it was given the status of a university.

1914 · The Aa Lake was constructed. In 1934 it was extended to the present size. It has become well-known far beyond Münster as a centre of water-sports (sailing-school and regattas). There are plans to extend it to the Steinburg or even as far as Haus Kump.

1930 · Dr. Heinrich Brüning, a native of Münster, became German Chancellor.

1933 · Clemens August, Count von Galen, minister of St. Lambert's Church was appointed Bishop of Münster.

1939 · The town's population rose to 141,059.

1941/5 · Wide-spread war-time damage in the town by bombing. 51 % of buildings were destroyed. 1119 Münster citizens and in addition 300–400 soldiers were killed in air raids. At the end of the war the town's population numbered 25,895.

1945 · The devastated town was occupied by the Allied Forces. The occupying authorities appointed a Provincial Government for Westphalia with its headquarters in Münster.

1946 · With the creation of the Province of North Rhine-Westphalia, Münster lost the supreme presidency. Its last Supreme President went to Düsseldorf as *Land* Prime Minister.

1949 · The Supreme Administrative Court of North Rhine-phalia was moved to Münster.

1952 · Münster became the seat of the Constitutional Court of Justice, the Supreme Court of the Province of North Rhine-Westphalia.

1953 · Autonomous government, centred in Münster, was re-established for Westphalia. Under the provisions for local government, the responsibilities of the Provincial Union were transferred to the Union of Westphalia-Lippe.

1966 · Münster's population totalled 200,000.

1968 · There are more than 22,000 students at the University and the two Colleges of Education; of these, more than 19,000 attend the University.

1974 · In the winter term of 1974/75 there were 34 773 students registered in Münster: 26 852 at the University, 4 721 at the Teachers' Training College, 3 200 at the Technical College.

1975 · In the communal restructuring process in North Rhine-Westphalia the District Münster-Land was dissolved. The communes Albachten, Amelsbüren, Angelmodde, Handorf, Hiltrup, St. Mauritz, Nienberge, Roxel and Wolbeck were united with Münster.

Thereby the town area was increased from 38.8 to 302.2 Hektar.

The number of inhabitants rose to 261 000.

The Budget for the enlarged town for the year 1975 was 587.7 million DM.

1976 · In the summer term of 1976 there were 36 342 students studying in Münster. Of these 28 342 were at the University, 4 800 at the Teachers' Training College, 3 211 at the Technical College and 244 at the National Academy of Music.

Source of illustrations: photographic archives of the Münster travel bureau 8, 10, 16, 29, 37, 39, 43, 45, 47, 48, 67, 69–72, 81, 93, 95, 100, 103, 105, 107, 109, 113, 125, 127, 128 / Christoph Bathe 59, 62, 76, 91, 124 / Anni Borgas 27, 96 / Eckhart Breider 17, 122, 123 / Hermann Greve 61 / Dr. Herwig Happe 10, 31, 33 / Landesdenkmalamt Westfalen (Hugo Schnautz) 50, 52, 55, 77, 83, 89, 113 / Landesmuseum für Kunst und Kulturgeschichte 25, 40–41 / Landesmuseum für Naturkunde (G. Hellmund) 111 / Rudolf Lindemann, Einbeck 119 / Walter Moog, Kettwig, aerial photograph 56–57 / N. Muddemann 15, 21, 28 / Carl Pohlschmidt 17, 65 / Albert Renger-Patsch, Wamel 19 / Wilhelm Rösch 53 / Paul Schwering 64 / Sten Woelm 98. The woodcut of the Messenger of Peace on p. 23 is at present in the Germanisches Museum in Nuremberg. The illustrations on page 39 are taken from the more recent edition of the Chronicle of the Anabaptists by Hermann Kerssenbroick.